SWISS PIONEERS
OF
SOUTHEASTERN OHIO

The Re-Discovered 1819 Settlements of
Jacob Tisher, Baron Rudolph de Steiguer, & Ludwig Gall
(plus John Joseph Labarthe in Louisiana)

By
Ernest Thode

CLEARFIELD

Copyright © 2017
Ernest Thode
All Rights Reserved

Published for Clearfield Company by
Genealogical Publishing Company
Baltimore Maryland
2017

ISBN 978-0-8063-5847-5

TABLE OF CONTENTS

i   Foreword

1   A Background of War and Misery

6   Jakob Tüscher (Jacob Tisher)

9   Baron Johann Rudolph von Steiger

12   Ludwig Gall

18   The French Connection:
        Jean (John) Joseph Labarthe

21   The Adventurous Journeys

46   Their Circumstances

64   The Lasting Legacy: Plans vs. Results

62   Passenger Lists (transcriptions)

82   The Individuals in their Communities

99   Summing Up

       Acknowledgements

       Passenger Lists (originals)

       Index

Foreword

I had to write this book. While researching my wife's Swiss-born ancestor Jacob Tisher, I discovered that little of his story had been discovered by historians; the related stories of two little-known Swiss groups who came to Ohio in 1819 had never been linked together. The president of the emigration society that brought them to America said in March 1819 that it was as good as dissolved, *"so gut wie aufgelöst."*[1] Some historians stated that the Swiss group dissolved when they arrived in America: *"In Amerika angekommen, löste sich die Gesellschaft sofort."*[2] According to others, it broke up *(ging auseinander)* soon afterwards; as Emil Lehmann concluded in 1861, *"Eine 1818 in Bern unter der Führung von Ludwig Gall, Hauptmann Steiger und Notar Reichenbach zusammengetretene Ansiedlungsgesellschaft ging bald nach ihrer Ankunft in America wieder auseinander."*[3]

It may be true that the formal society had split up, but I knew that a significant group of people arrived and stayed here. Henry Howe's *History of Ohio* highlights Jacob Tisher's party that made the first German and Swiss settlements in Monroe County.[4] There is still a substantial Swiss colony in Monroe County, Ohio, stemming from this emigrant group of Jacob Tisher. I had seen their genealogies. Why were they so little known?

After I discovered a 989-page book by Ludwig Gall in German about this journey in 2013, a real breakthrough, I became eager to get a more complete picture, and so I turned to a wide-ranging variety of sources. Assisted by supportive and resourceful researchers, librarians, and archivists, I have tried to "connect the dots." Each

---

[1] Reichenbach, Samuel, in his report of 9 April 1819, Staatsarchiv Bern, BB XIIIa 151, 30-31.

[2] Stegmann, Carl, and Hugo Lindermann, *Handbuch des Socialismus*, (Zürich: J. Verlags-Magazin (J. Schabelitz), 1897), 278.

[3] Lehmann, Emil, *Die deutsche Auswanderung*, (Berlin: Georg Reimer, 1861), 32.

[4] Howe, Henry, *Historical Collections of Ohio*, (Columbus, Ohio: Henry Howe & Son, 1891), Vol. II, 533.

new find led to eye-opening insights and more leads. Piecing them all together, I saw how people's decisions to emigrate are influenced by innumerable factors such as wars, extreme weather, disease, poverty, social class, legal status, employment, availability of transportation, and even romance. These are the life-changing stories of real people, with worries and shortcomings and dreams and successes and failures, whether they be rural laborers, craftsmen, burghers, or aristocrats. As it turns out, quite a few events seemingly lost to history had been documented, some of them in surprising detail, serendipitously surfacing through family histories and letters, described in their own words. The grand history and world-shaking events that we study about in school are the sum total of all these mini-histories of countless individual decisions.

These settlers repeatedly faced all kinds of life-and-death situations. At home the Swiss faced oppression, wars, starvation, and epidemics. Along their journeys they faced dangers from thieves, the perilous Rhine passage, rough toll takers, delays and evil shippers in the harbor, storms on the ocean voyage, and an armed and crazed passenger. In America they faced an impending yellow fever outbreak, sending children out to beg for food, primeval forests to clear, a house fire, and wild animals. These Swiss pioneers have their own histories. They persisted and endured. Their stories deserve to be told. This book may help fill out a chapter in the history of Swiss emigration.

Our Swiss immigrants of 1819 played a role in the history of the world. They faced many innovative concepts such as the U.S. Constitution, the Napoleonic Code, the Northwest Ordinance, and the Treaty of Vienna, new religious denominations such as German Methodist and Apostolic Christian, and colonization societies. Surprisingly, many well-known names documented within one or two degrees of separation crop up in their far-reaching and intriguing story: famous Americans such as Daniel Boone, Cornstalk, navigator Zadock Cramer, orator Edward Everett, Benjamin Franklin, Captain John Paul Jones, Francis Scott Key, Dr. Benjamin Rush, and Commodore Cornelius Vanderbilt; Presidents George Washington & John Quincy Adams and Vice-Presidents Aaron Burr & Daniel Tompkins; Europeans including Napoleon, ex-

Spanish King Joseph Bonaparte, Harman Blennerhassett, the "French Five Hundred" of Gallipolis, Ambassador Albert Gallatin, botanist Albrecht von Haller, Lord Byron, Karl Marx, Prince Maximilian of Wied, chocolatier Philippe Suchard, and Swiss patriot Heinrich Zschokke; and the prominent Ohio pioneer families of Ames, Barber, Fearing, Jewett, Nye, Putnam, Sproat, and Tupper. There are allusions to other Swiss and German settlements in Brazil, Illinois, Indiana, Louisiana, New York, North Carolina, Ohio, and Pennsylvania, and unrealized settlements in Arkansas Territory, Missouri, and (West) Virginia. Many questions were answered by unforeseen new findings, but I was forced to rethink many long-held notions.

A Background of War and Misery

Illustration of Battle of Grauholz 1798, by Karl Minde ca 1870, after Friedrich Walthard

In the early 1800s a number of events beyond their control brought suffering Swiss settlers into two frontier regions of Ohio to build a new life in the New World, where countless descendants live today. Switzerland was in turmoil after an invasion by France in 1798, when forced quartering of occupying soldiers led to food shortages, hard times, and disease. The conquering French plundered 6.7 million francs in gold, seized 4 million francs from the Bernese treasury, and, adding insult to injury, charged Bern with the expense of their invasion.[1] The new French-sponsored Helvetic Republic of 1798-1803 that replaced Wilhelm Tell's ancient Swiss Confederation of 1291 soon fell apart; for Canton Bern it had meant military

---

[1] Rohrbaugh/Rohrbach, Louis Bunker, *Men of Bern: The 1798 Bürgerverzeichnisse of Canton Bern, Switzerland,* (Rockport, Maine: Picton Press, 1999), Vol. 1, Introduction, xxiii.

subjugation by France. Impoverished farmers in Canton Bern and other cantons rose up against the French in the 1802 *Stecklikrieg* (Stick War), with no weapons but farm tools such as pitchforks, brooms, hoes, rakes, and wooden clubs. Switzerland's celebrated neutral independence was reinstated by the Congress of Vienna in 1815, but the Confederation had a military obligation requiring 2 per cent of men from each canton to serve.

Conditions in central Europe had been topsy-turvy since the French Revolution. Royalty was either decapitated or deposed. Everywhere, soldiers blamed France for the death and devastation of war. The first estate, the clergy, deplored their weakened influence after their properties were looted and confiscated and they criticized the general lack of religion in a new secular society. The second estate, nobles, detested an uppity bourgeoisie that no longer knew its place. Politicians grumbled about individual nobles. The third estate, everybody else, blamed businesses and banks for high prices and inflation. Despite nominal equality under the law, not much changed for poor people; they remained impoverished and still sought subsistence for their families.

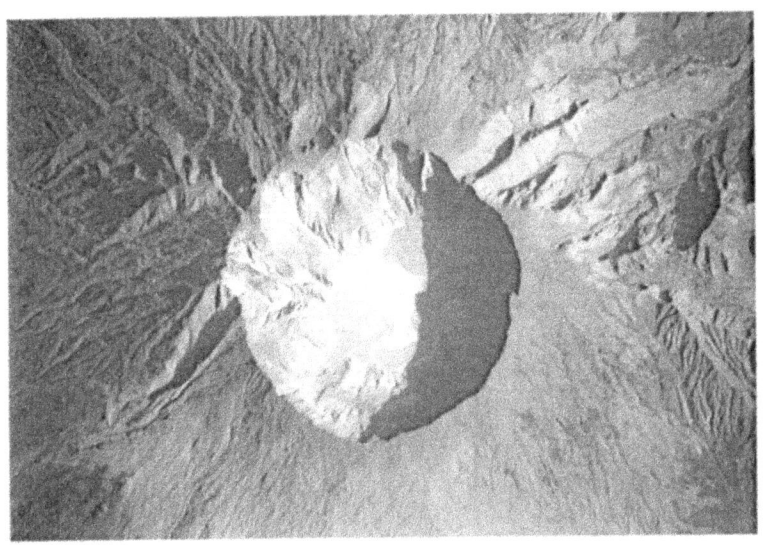

Tambora caldera: NASA Earth Observatory

The eventual "push factor" for many Swiss emigrants between 1816 and 1819–their last straw–was the climatic effect from the massive eruption of Mount Tambora, a stratovolcano on Sumbawa Island in the Dutch East Indies (now Indonesia) lasting more or less from April 10 to April 17, 1815. It is rather arcanely classified in modern scientific literature as a "VEI-7 super-colossal Ultra-Plinian" explosion, which discharged 38 cubic miles of deposits and left a crater 3.7 miles in diameter. The huge blast sent up an ash column reaching the stratosphere that released reflective sulfate ions through the northern hemisphere, clouding the sky, obscuring the sun's warmth for more than a year, and triggering a "volcanic winter."[2] An outbreak of hailstorms, cloudbursts, and floods occurred throughout Europe, creating a deadly pattern of crop failures, even greater famine, abject poverty, disease, and inflation, sparking food riots, arson, and looting in cities. In North America 1816 was called "the year without a summer" and "Eighteen hundred and froze to death" for good reason, though the actual cause was unknown at the time in both Europe and America.

---

[2] D'Arcy Wood, Gillen, *Tambora: The Eruption That Changed the World*, (Princeton, NJ: Princeton University Press, 2014), 41 and passim.

Swiss seeking food during the famine, courtesy of Toggenburger Museum, Lichtensteig, Switzerland

In Switzerland the average temperature fell 2.5º C. (4.5º F.) below normal in 1816.[3] There was snow and frost in every month of the year, it rained 50 days during May through July, unripe grapes were harvested in November, blight ruined the potato crop, herbs and roots were used for soup, people gathered grass beside their cattle, and standard bread loaves were reduced in size.[4] As a result of all the snowfall, a major flood occurred in 1817.[5] People desperately looked for a way out to avoid starvation. Would-be European emigrants left the lands bordering the Rhine, their most accessible exit route, during the hunger years 1816 and 1817, packing all available ships bound for America, but with the result that thousands left in the harbors had no choice for the winter but to freeze, starve,

---

[3] www.naturwissenschaften.ch/service/news/37952-hungersnot-in-der-schweiz-nach-vulkanausbruch-1815----sind-wir-heute-fuer-eine-solche-katastrophe-geruestet-

[4] Gratz, Delbert, *Bernese Anabaptists and their American Descendants*, (Goshen, Indiana: The Mennonite Historical Society, 1994), 110.

[5] www.naturwissenschaften.ch/service/news/37952-hungersnot-in-der-schweiz-nach-vulkanausbruch-1815---sind-wir-heute-fuer-eine-solche-katastrophe-geruestet-

or go back home as paupers, without provisions, without legal protection, lice-infested, and in rags. A typhus epidemic in 1818 was transmitted by would-be emigrants of 1817 who returned home. All of this was occurring during a hiatus provided for in the Treaty of Vienna during which persons from formerly French-controlled areas such as Canton Bern theoretically were allowed to travel freely from 1815 to 1821.

The "pull" of America, even for immigrants arriving at the time of the Panic of 1819 in the U.S., was strong: plenty of cheap land, raw natural resources, personal freedom, job opportunities, open spaces instead of Europe's overcrowding, no tithes or compulsory service owed to rulers, no oppressive state church, and a chance to earn citizenship and the right to vote for one's leaders. Governments had to relax anti-emigration regulations and in fact they were glad to cull what they considered overpopulation, especially people they deemed undesirable. The best-known example is that several Swiss cantons paid the passage for 1,682 Swiss (946 men and 736 women) in 261 families to leave for Brazil beginning July 11, 1819. Unfortunately, their Novo Friburgo settlement fell apart by 1825 as a result of 449 deaths at sea, illness, poverty, a poor choice of location, and local prejudice against foreigners.[6] Our immigrants to North America, however, were not government-sponsored; they were funded by a newly-formed private colonization society.

---

[6] *Archiv für Sippenforschung und alle verwandten Gebiete*, (Limburg an der Lahn: C. A. Starke, 1931), Vol. 8, 86.

Photo from Melba Gorby Beard, descendant;
signature from Tisher letter to American Mission Board

Jakob Tüscher (later Jacob Tisher), banished from Canton Bern in March 1819, led a group of emigrants that wound up in Belmont and Monroe Counties, Ohio. Jakob had a hard early life. According to Bernese law, he was born out of wedlock in 1777 but was legitimized in 1790. During the devastating Battle of Grauholz on March 5, 1798, in Tüscher's hard-hit home commune of Büren zum Hof, an Anna Tüscher, widow of a Hans Tüscher, was one of the residents who died, along with schoolmaster Hans Schneider, Johannes Schneider, woodworker Jakob Landolf, and guardsmen Jakob Messerli and Niklaus Eberhardt, a father of six.[7] (A Schneider family and an Eberhardt family would also leave with him 21 years later.) Girls as young as 14 were assaulted by French marauders and 46 horses

---

[7] "Notizen über einige Todte und Verwundete am 5. März," *Berner Taschenbuch*, (Bern, Switzerland: Vol. 40), 140.

were commandeered in Büren zum Hof alone, leaving just one poor old workhorse in the village. Reformed church sexton Niklaus Tüscher, a namesake of Tüscher's father, was killed by the French invaders in the local parish community, Limpach.[8]

Jakob first worked as a weaver in French-speaking Payerne/Peterlingen, Canton Vaud/Waadt, but from 1806 to 1816 he acted as a legal agent in Mülchi and Reiben (now Büren an der Aare, Canton Bern); his files of debts and property and personal correspondence for those years are preserved in the Swiss Federal Archives in Bern.[9] In 1810 he applied for citizenship in Büren an der Aare, not to be confused with his nearby home town Büren zum Hof (both places are in Canton Bern). Swiss citizenship, with all that it entails, resides in the male hereditary family's commune (based on residence in 1672) rather than with the national government or in the current residence, and exemplifies the principle so simply expressed by Robert Frost: "Home is the place where, when you have to go there, they have to take you in."[10] Büren an der Aare, closely guarding its citizenships and its finances, refused his application to become a *Hintersäß* (legal inhabitant without voting rights) because of his bad name, his debts, and his two children born to different women before his divorce. Büren an der Aare clearly did not want to "have to take him in."

Tüscher had fathered an extramarital child with Elisabeth Arn in 1809, finally was divorced from Maria Brossy (each had filed charges of adultery against the other) in 1812, and produced five more children in six and a half years with his wife/housekeeper Katharina Winterberger, getting the couple back in trouble with Bernese authorities when their residence commune of Reiben reverted back to Bern after a period of French control. Jakob was sentenced to

---

[8] "Notizen," 142.
[9] Staatsarchiv Kanton Bern, Bezirksarchiv Büren, A 437 (1806-1816), and A 438 (1806-1816).
[10] Frost, Robert, "The Death of the Hired Man," *North of Boston*, (New York: H. Holl and Company, 1915).

prison for three years and Katharina for one.[11] After that, Jakob and his outcast family were unquestionably ready to take a leap of faith and make their exodus from Bern for a promised land.

---

[11] *Manual des Chorgerichts der Stadt und Republik Bern,* (Bern, Switzerland: Stadt und Republik Bern, March 28, 1816), 131-133.

The Baron's personal signet with the black von Steiger coat of arms, photo by Alexandra de Steiguer

Coming from a much loftier milieu, **Freiherr (= Baron) Johann Rudolph von Steiger** (the family later used de Steiguer when the son Rodolphe reinstated a previously-used French form) led a parallel group of Swiss colonists who wound up in Athens County, Ohio, in 1819. He had also run afoul of severe Bernese marriage laws. The von Steiger family name was the foremost in Switzerland. His family belonged to one of the 13 leading Bernese patrician societies, the *Ober-Gerwern*, an elite ruling-class club which developed out of the tanner and leatherworker's guild, with legal standing equal to a city. In 1796 the Sovereign Council had 22 von Steigers/de Steiguers, the most prominent family, followed next by 15 von Wattenwyls, 14 von Jenners, 12 von Tscharners, and 11 von

Graffenrieds.[12] The Baron's line, v. Steiger de Gran(d)son, ennobled by the King of Prussia in 1714 for Christoph v. Steiger's help in securing Neuchâtel as a Swiss foothold for Prussia,[13] has a rising *(steigend)* black ibex in its coat of arms, with the Latin motto *Vive ut vives* (Live life to the fullest).[14] The Castle at Chillon on Lake Geneva, immortalized in a famous poem by Lord Byron, has a stained-glass window displaying Christoph's coat of arms. Christoph was the Baron's great-great-great-uncle. The last mayor of the City and Republic of Bern in 1798 was Niklaus Friedrich v. Steiger of this branch, the Baron's second cousin twice removed, their common ancestor being Emanuel Steiger (1615-1670).[15] The von Steiger dynasty had intermarried for centuries with the noble de Graffenried family that founded the New Bern, North Carolina, settlement in 1709; the Baron's de Graffenried great-aunt cared for his three children in botanist Albrecht von Haller II's former studio in Geneva after his divorce. In Ohio his children were tutored by his cousin Colonel Emanuel Gabriel May, formerly of the Swiss Guard in Holland, who taught school subjects and instilled discipline, table manners, courteous speech, and proper carriage.

Like so many Swiss men employed in foreign military service *(Reislaufen)*–the nobility as officers, ordinary soldiers as mercenaries–the Baron had served, namely as Captain of the Guard for Karl Friedrich, the Grand-Duke of Baden, in Karlsruhe, who gave him an ornate snuff box for his service. The Baron also was one of the Swiss officers opposing Napoleon's invasion in 1798 and as a result was imprisoned in a French fortress[16] near Strasbourg for 18 months. Though a patrician with the most powerful pedigree in Bern, Rudolph had scandalously married and divorced commoner Wilhelmine Müller, daughter of a gardener at the Grand-Duke's palace grounds, who had gotten into a relationship with her

---

[12] de Steiguer, Johann Rudolph (b 1827), *History of the de Steiguer Family*, (Athens, Ohio: self-published, 1888), 9.

[13] Hoskins, 67.

[14] Hoskins, 151.

[15] von Steiger, Kurt, *Stammbaum der Familie v. Steiger mit dem schwarzem Steinbock im Wappen* (Bern, Switzerland: manuscript, undated.)

[16] de Steiguer (1888), 14.

husband-to-be Samuel Stettler, followed by Steiger's own dishonorable love affair with Magdalena, daughter of his loyal miller Jacob Stalder.[17] In Switzerland, von Steiger was a member of the ruling class and had no other gainful profession. He was in an untenable position, alienated from his family. When grain became unavailable after being used up by invading armies and as relief for the starving poor, the Baron sold his flour mill in Canton Bern and brought Magdalena's whole extended Stalder clan with him as the core of his expatriate party. The Baron regarded Stalder as "very honest, upright, trusty, and most excellent ... in every respect."[18] Like Tüscher, Baron von Steiger had decided for a drastic change, a fresh start with lovely Magdalena and his new "Papa" and family in America, a land with unlimited potential.

---

[17] *Schweizerisches Geschlechterbuch/Almanach Généalogique* Suisse (Bern: C. F. Lendorff, 1907), 547-551.

[18] de Steiguer (1888), 18.

The Vision of a New Beginning

Lithograph of Ludwig Gall by unknown graphic artist,
Illustrirter Kalender, vol. 15 (1860), 68

Ludwig Gall (Heinrich Ludwig Lambert Gall), our third major character, born in Aldenhoven, but a resident of Trier in Prussia's newly acquired province of Rhineland, was the man behind the emigration plan, an unlikely organizer of two Swiss settlements. He had studied at the secondary school in Aachen/Aix-la-Chapelle in the Rhineland where his uncle Franz Peter Gall, the headmaster, taught liberal civic values, and Ludwig became a government clerk out of an instilled sense of public responsibility.[19] Gall became a promoter of American colonization, having seen first-hand the life-or-death predicament of thousands of would-be German and Swiss emigrants forced to go back to their homes because there were no more ships

---

[19] Monz, Heinz, *Ludwig Gall: Leben und Werk*, (Trier, Germany: NCO-Verlag Neu, 1979), 5.

available. He witnessed their reverse exodus at his several posts along the Rhine and Moselle valleys while serving as a clerk for the French government, the Russian military, and the Prussian king. Out of a sense of conscience, he voluntarily gave up his Prussian citizenship and government clerkship on February 12, 1819, to attempt to launch his colonization society.[20] Gall believed in his ideas so strongly that he wound up bringing along his parents and his young bride on a perilous trans-Atlantic voyage, hardly her vision of a leisurely honeymoon cruise.

We can read all about it because Gall had a penchant for writing. As a schoolboy prodigy he wrote compulsively, so much that his parents and teachers did not know what to do with him. He kept meticulous notes of his travel experiences, filling two volumes with 989 pages about his emigration and return published in 1822. Without his writings, we would be in the dark about much of this history.

Most emigrants from German lands in this era, especially Catholics, were choosing to go to eastern areas of Europe, such as the Austro-Hungarian Empire, which actively recruited settlers. But people living near the Rhine, especially Protestants, preferred to sail to New York or Philadelphia by way of the Rhenish seaports of Rotterdam, Antwerp, or Amsterdam, or by making the trek across France to the port of Le Havre. The United States, especially the northern states and the Northwest Territory (particularly Ohio, Indiana, and Illinois), with no slavery or tropical diseases, had become the destination of choice for daring Europeans like Gall. America's attraction was as a land of opportunity, a new start as redemptioners for those in dire straits in Europe. Residents of the Rhine valley had heard numerous American rags-to-riches stories from local lore. Some of their former neighbors had relocated in the 18th century to William Penn's tolerant refuge of Pennsylvania, though some of the success stories undoubtedly were exaggerated by returning "newlanders" who earned commissions by indenturing emigrants.[21]

---

[20] Gall, Ludwig, *Meine Auswanderung nach den Vereingten-Staaten in Nord-Amerika im Frühjahr 1819 und meine Rückkehr nach der Heimath im Winter 1820* (Trier, Germany: F. A. Gall, 1822), vol. I, 44.

[21] Wokeck, Marianne S., *Trade in Strangers: The Beginnings of Mass Migrations to North America*, (State College, PA: Penn State Press, 1999), 163.

Gall, whose father was a wine merchant and innkeeper, and whose new father-in-law, Dr. Jakob Josef Will(e)wers(ch), of Trier in the Moselle wine region, owned a vineyard estate, the 32-acre *Kleeburger Hof*,[22] had read about the wine-making settlements in America of Swiss brothers Jean Jacques and Jean François DuFour of Châtelard, Canton Vaud, in Kentucky in a region where Switzers had previously settled and later along the Ohio River in Indiana. Emulating them, Gall tried to establish a society to colonize emigrants in 1818 in Trier in the Rhineland, only lately under Prussian rule, but the new government refused to authorize it. Gall's local friends, admirers of Baron von Gagern, then had to turn their attentions away from Prussia to a group of Hanoverian farmers who settled Vandalia, Illinois.[23]

In 1817 Baron Hans Christoph Ernst von Gagern had sent Baron Moritz von Fürstenwärther, his cousin and orphaned ward, to Philadelphia to investigate conditions on ships and in America for colonization from Europe. His report was published in Europe in 1818 and became the impetus for Gall's society, which Gall had called the *Gagernsche Gesellschaft* after Baron von Gagern. An enthusiastic Baron von Fürstenwärther requested help from the United States government for resettling distressed refugees, possibly hoping for a U.S. government position for his trouble. In the reply, with cautiously chosen words, Secretary of State John Quincy Adams told him not to anticipate any special favors. "The government of the United States has never adopted any measure to encourage or invite emigrants from any part of Europe." Adams refused to suggest the states might subsidize them: "Emigrants ... are not to expect favors from the governments. They are to expect, if they choose to become citizens, equal rights with those of the natives of the country. They are to expect, if affluent, to possess the means of making their property productive, with moderation, and with safety;—if indigent, but industrious, honest and frugal, the means of obtaining easy and

---

[22] Zimmer, Theresia, "Der Hof Kleeburg," in *Neues Trierisches Jahrbuch* (Trier, Germany: Verein Trierisch e.V.,1969), 65-72.

[23] Friesen, Gerhard, "Moritz von Fürstenwärther and America," in *Yearbook of German-American Studies*, Vol. 16, (Lawrence, Kansas: University of Kansas, 1981), 74-75.

comfortable subsistence for themselves and their families."[24] Meanwhile, though, inspired by von Fürstenwärther's report, Gall had liquidated his possessions and advertised throughout Europe in 1818 for investors in his private emigration society with a detailed proposal for a planned community to be called *Rosenau*.[25] Baron von Steiger himself had inserted announcements in Swiss newspapers to form a colony between the 38th and 39th parallel in Missouri, [26] and responded to Gall's like-minded advertisements. With a tight timeline for a spring departure, Steiger's emigration commission was formed on February 2, 1819, in Bern.[27]

Gall's and Steiger's goals overlapped, and the combined Swiss-Rhineland Emigration Commission, hastily cobbled together by correspondence, convened on March 16, 1819, in Bern. It consisted of the officers:
President Samuel **Reichenbach**, of Bern, a notary, listed by Gall in abbreviated form as *Herr R.* [misinterpreted by Edward Everett as Mr. N.];
Vice-President Ludwig **Küpfer**, of Bern, an architect and hospital commissioner, [Gall writes it Kupfer];
Secretary Beat Ludwig Meßmer (**Messmer**), of Bern, an attorney and historian, the Bern municipal archivist, who was the agent for an

---

[24] Adams, John Quincy, "Emigration to the U. States," *Niles' Weekly Register*, (Baltimore, H. Niles, April 29, 1820), Vol. 18, 157-158. (Letter from Washington, DC, June 4, 1819, in response to letter of Morris von Furstenwaerther dated April 22, 1819, in Philadelphia.)

[25] Gall, Ludwig, "Aufruf zur Bildung menschenfreundlicher Vereine für eine der wichtigsten Angelegenheiten der Zeit und der Menschheit," proposal for a humanitarian colonization society (23 Jan 1819), and "Auszug aus einem Entwurf zur Anlegung einer Colonie in den vereinigten Staaten von Nord-Amerika," a detailed outline for a colony in North America, in *Isis, oder enzyklopädische Zeitung* (Jena: Ludwig Oken, June 4, 1819, Heft 3, No. 32), 498-507.

[26] Natsch, Rudolf Arnold, *Die Haltung eidgenössischer und kantolaner Behörden in der Auswanderungsfrage 1803-1874* (Bern, Switzerland: P.G. Keller, 1960), 39.

[27] *Der aufrichtige und wohlerfhrene Schweizer-Bote* (Aarau, Switzerland: Sauerländer, February 25, 1819), Vol 16, No. 8, 62-63.

1817 famine relief commission that procured much-needed grain from Heilbronn, Württemberg, itself hard-hit;[28]

Commissioner Ludwig **Gall**, *in absentia*, the lone German member, of Trier in the Rhineland, who had sold his possessions and obtained investors, busy working out advance transportation arrangements in ports;

Commissioner Jean Joseph **Labarthe**, of Geneva, a well-to-do French-speaking cotton goods manufacturer, navigator, merchant, and trader;

Baron Auguste de **Vasserot** /August von **Wasserroth**, of Vincy, Canton Vaud, who was ruined by the French Revolution and provided a refuge for French *emigrés* from Robespierre's reign of terror in his *chateau*, whom Reichenbach praised as adding credence for the plan, but an eccentric who was perhaps only a figurehead or declined to serve (named a commissioner on February 6, 1819, but absent for the March meeting);[29] and

Commissioner Captain Rudolph **von Steiger** de Gran(d)son, of Bern, a baron and military officer [called *Hauptmann v. ---g---* by Gall, one of many confusing concealments of names commonly used by Gall, as well as by other writers of the era]. —

Four of the commissioners, namely Gall, Labarthe, Reichenbach, and von Steiger, came to America, supervising their charges, despite diverging motivations and mutual distrust. There were rivalries and clashes between strong personalities. Each seemed to believe he was in charge: Gall, using von Gagern's idea of a planned American German colonization, who made the advance shipping arrangements, the plan's initiator from the Rhineland; Labarthe, hoping to develop a rich international cotton trading enterprise, the group's contact man with his fellow Genevan and boyhood acquaintance, U.S. Ambassador Albert Gallatin; Reichenbach, elected the president of the commission, who drew up a colony on paper and dispatched the orders to the others; and von Steiger, the top-echelon nobleman and imperious military commander, basically mobilizing a foreign expedition, expecting to govern his North American settlement of

---

[28] Erne, Emil, "Das Stadtarchiv Bern: Geschichte–Standort–Bestände," in *Berner Zeitschrift für Geschichte* (Bern, Switzerland: 2010), No. 3, 12-13.

[29] Gall I, 42.

Swiss. Each recognized the character flaws in the others but not his own.[30] Predictably, in America the four egos all scattered and went their separate ways after legal wrangling. Jakob Tüscher, too, had his own payment disputes with Gall. He intended to take his assemblage of Swiss families to a slave state, Virginia, which was an abhorrent idea to Gall. Gall's and Tüscher's groups also went their separate ways, though ironically Tüscher settled in Ohio, a free state, in the end, and Gall's contracted servants took American freedom all too literally and left him.

Between 1816 and 1819 Canton Bern issued nearly 160 passports for North America. Many of them were for Mennonites, who reported good experiences in America back to Switzerland.[31] In 1817 a colony of six Swiss Mennonite families from the Jura region (of Peter Lehmann, Isaac Sommer, Ulrich Lehmann, David Kilchhofer, Benedict Schrag, and Hans Burkholder) had settled in Sonne(n)berg (now Kidron), Wayne County, Ohio. In late July and early August 1819 the Tisher and de Steiguer parties arrived in America, beating Gall's noble friends to the punch by a year. By the time Ferdinand Ernst's colony of Hanoverians settled at Vandalia, Illinois, and the government-sponsored Swiss colonization group landed in Brazil in 1820, Gall's efforts had already produced two German-speaking Swiss settlements in North America that left their imprint in three Ohio counties, if not exactly the full-fledged colony that he projected. Another family eventually went to Louisiana. Altogether there were only 31 total Swiss who entered the U.S. counted in fiscal year 1820, the first year of records, but each of our two 1819 Ohio groups outnumbered the next year's total.[32]

---

[30] *Isis von Oken*, (Jena, Germany: Lorenz Oken, in der Expedition, 1824), Band 1, Heft 2, 203.

[31] *Allgemeine Zeitung, Mit Allerhöchsten Privilegien*, (Tübingen, Germany: Johann Friedrich Cotta, August 25, 1819), 2.

[32] *Letter from the Secretary of State, with a Transcript of the List of Passengers Who Arrived in the United States from the 1st October, 1819, to the 30th September, 1820*, (Washington, D.C., Gales & Seaton, 1821), 16th Congress, 2nd Session, Senate Document 118, Serial No. 145, 24.

The French Connection

Pierre Labarthe Coat of Arms

Jean Joseph Labarthe was the emigration commissioner who spoke only French, forcing the marine trial proceedings to be conducted in French. His father Pierre Labarthe, a Protestant saddler, was born in Tonneins, Guyenne, Département Lot-et-Garonne in southwestern

France in 1735, and moved to the Huguenot refuge city of Geneva, Switzerland, home town of Jean Calvin the Reformer, where he became a new citizen on October 8, 1759. Emigrant Jean Joseph married Jeanne Eleonore Chollet in Geneva. He was one of the four commissioners escorting their emigrants, hoping to utilize his skills as a navigator and mapmaker. His four children who went to Louisiana were François Philippe, a doctor in Assumption Parish (=County), Louisiana, who left 10 children; Jean Joseph, Jr., a navigator and steamboat captain on Louisiana waterways until the U.S. Civil War, who had 7 children; Suzanne Marguerite, an unmarried plantation owner in Assumption Parish (=County), Louisiana; and Jean Auguste, a shoemaker, first residing with his siblings, initially at Susanne Marguerite's plantation and then with Jean Joseph, Jr., in New Orleans. These children in birth order and their families are:

Suzanne Marguerite Labarthe, Protestant, born 6 Mar 1795 Geneva, Switzerland, unmarried, plantation owner, died between her writing a will in Assumption Parish, Louisiana, on 13 Dec 1863 and her will being proved in the Second District of New Orleans on 11 Jan 1864.

Jean Joseph (J. J.) Labarthe, Jr., born 2 Jul 1802 Geneva, Switzerland, steamboat captain,
married
Marie Delzine Landry, of Bayou Teche, Louisiana.
Children:
Delphine, born 13 Apr 1830 in St. Martin Parish, married Charles L. Hardie, a steamboat clerk and captain.
John Alexander, born 24 Nov 1832 in St. Martin Parish, a clerk in New Orleans, Louisiana, married Anaise Elie.
John Joseph, born 13 Mar 1835 in St. Martin Parish, a steamboat pilot.
Philippe A. Labarthe, born 19 Oct 1837, a clerk, married Camille Perrot.
Marie Louise Claire, born 3 Sep 1840, baptized 4 Sep 1840.
Louise Caroline, born ca 20 Oct 1842 in St. Martin Parish. (??)
Ernest Leonard, born ca 20 Oct 1842 in St. Martin Parish, married Louisa M. Fraitas.

[Dr.] François Philippe Labarthe, born 1 Mar 1804 Geneva, Switzerland, baptized 13 Apr 1804 Plainpalais, Switzerland (Reformed),
married 12 Jun 1832 in Assumption Roman Catholic parish, Plattenville, Louisiana,
Aglee Martin, daughter of plantation owner Joseph Richard Martin and Marguerite Verret, and coincidentally granddaughter of a Jean Etienne Labarthe, whose family has its origin in Granger parish, Diocese of Agin, France.
Children:
Philippe, born ca May 1833, buried 27 Aug 1834 Ascension Roman Catholic parish, Donaldsonville, LA.
Marie Aglee, born 28 Dec 1835, baptized 6 May 1837 Assumption RC parish.
Therese Emelie, born 20 Feb 1837, baptized 6 May 1837 Assumption RC parish.
Philippe, born 25 Jul 1838, baptized 25 Jul 1838 Ascension RC parish.
Joseph Numa, born 20 Aug 1840, baptized 10 Oct 1840 Assumption RC parish.
Paulene Eleonore, born ca. 1843
Marie Clara, born 16 Jan 1845, baptized 30 Jul 1845 Ascension RC parish.
Marguerite Alice, born 9 Dec 1846, baptized 3 Jan 1847 St. Elizabeth Roman Catholic parish, Paincourtville, LA.
Jean Alphonse, born 22 Jan 1849, baptized 23 Jan 1849 St. Elizabeth RC parish.
Felicien Adele, born 22 Dec 1850, baptized 6 Feb 1851 St. Elizabeth RC parish.
Marie Laura, born 15 Dec 1853, baptized 23 Dec 1853 St. Elizabeth RC parish.

Jean Auguste Labarthe, born 21 Aug 1806 Geneva, Switzerland, a shoemaker, unmarried, died 12 Nov 1869 New Orleans, LA, buried Cypress Grove Cemetery, New Orleans, LA.

The Adventurous Journeys

Jakob Tüscher took his Swiss party from Bern down the Aare and Rhine by flatboat, setting out April 12, 1819, which was Easter Monday. 1819, like 1816 and 1817, was another busy year for emigration. During 1818 there had been a large dropoff in numbers of Swiss due to the deadly disease and malnutrition of hundreds of Aargau emigrants aboard the "Aprill" from Amsterdam to New Castle, Delaware. Between April 17 and May 31 there were 683 emigrants passing through the confluence of the Main and Rhine at Mainz from Württemberg (including 378 Separatists), 192 from Baden, 171 Swiss, 60 Rhine Bavarians, 28 Rhine Hessians, and 28 Alsatians.[33]

---

[33] *Allgemeine Zeitung mit allerhöchsten Privilegien*, (München: 1819 No. 163, 12 June 1819), 652.

Illustration of Binger Loch by Clarkson Stanfield

The mind-jolting journey down the Rhine from Basel to Dordrecht, with the crowding on deck, the belligerent gun-toting toll collectors, the treacherous narrows at the Binger Loch, and the legendary hazards of the rocky Lorelei, was described by Niklaus Fankhauser as even worse than the hardships of the ocean voyage, when he was knocked down by a wave.[34] Luckily, they barely escaped the clampdown by the Prussian ministry of police against transitory emigrants of May 21 and the specifically anti-Swiss decree of June 14.[35] There were dropouts along the way, which particularly irked Gall, who wanted larger numbers to justify hiring the ships and fulfill his humanitarian goals.

---

[34] Harshbarger, Wilma R., *Family Genealogy of Christian Marty, Barbara Ruegsegger*, (Atwood, IL: Wilma Harshbarger, 1984), 8.

[35] Prussian Royal Government of the Rhineland, Decrees No. 137, dated May 21, 1819, and 159, dated June 14, 1819, promulgated in *Amtsblatt der Königlichen Preußischen Regierung*, (Düsseldorf: Königlich Preußische Regierung, 1819), No. 34, 255 and No. 40, 310.

The "*Eugénie*," Ludwig Gall, *Meine Auswanderung*,
Vol. 1, inside front cover

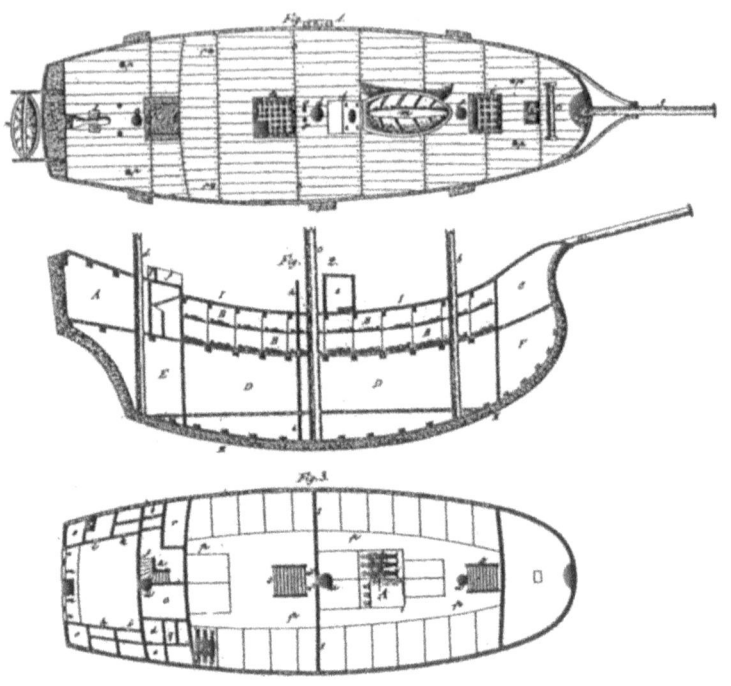

Top, Side, & Cross-Section Views of *Eugénie*,
Meine Auswanderung, Vol. 1, inside front cover

The emigrants with cash could buy all manner of supplies at a "Grocery Store" in the port at Antwerp: pickled meat, dried beans, sardines, sausages, smoked ham, butter, sauerkraut, smoked tongue, canned foods, flour, rice, chocolate, coffee, sugar, salted fish, wine and brandy in bottles and casks, brushes, fine sand, ropes, sailor shirts, maps, lanterns, candles, soup spoons, ironware, whale oil, flax, spyglasses, tin and pewter containers, snuff cases, books, quadrants, pipes, sea boots, straw hats, playing cards, cooking pots, toys, straw mats, trusses, mirrors, mattresses, bird cages, writing tools, plus hundreds of other items, according to Gall.[36]

Gall's contracted rations were Sundays ½ lb. of beef, ½ lb. rice, Mondays ½ lb. rice, ½ lb. flour, Tuesdays ½ lb. bacon, ½ lb. peas, Wednesdays ½ lb. beef, ½ lb. rice, Thursdays ½ lb. bacon, ½ lb.

---

[36] Gall I, 89.

beans, Fridays ¾ lb. dried cod, 4 lbs. of potatoes, Saturdays ½ lb. meat, ½ lb. barley, plus 1 lb. butter, 1 lb. cheese, 7 lbs. of zwieback (which doesn't turn moldy at sea), 1 liter of brandy, 1 vat of vinegar, salt, pepper, bottled water, and for the first 3 weeks a liter of beer a day. The provisions decided on by the elected traveler representatives were somewhat different: 4,200 lbs. of zwieback instead of 5,200 lbs., less flour but more rice than agreed upon, and no beans but triple the peas. The final totals, based on 105 passengers and allowing for a 10-week supply, were 1,400 lbs. of beef, 1,050 lbs. rice, 500 lbs. flour, 500 lbs. bacon, 1,050 lbs. peas, 525 lbs. dried cod, 9,000 lbs. potatoes, 300 lbs. barley, 637 lbs. butter, 712 lbs. cheese, 5,737 lbs. zwieback, 663 bottles of brandy, 600 jugs of vinegar, 360 lbs. salt, and 5 lbs. pepper.[37] The steerage passengers were bedded three to a 72" x 42" compartment instead of the typical four or five, so their billets were less cramped than most other passenger ships. The cost for hiring their ship was 14,800 francs or $37.60 fare per passenger plus 8,510 francs or $21.62 per person for provisions.[38]

By this time, on the other side of the ocean, the U.S. Congress had passed an immigration law on March 2 mandating a maximum of 2 passengers per 5 tons, each with 60 gallons of water, 100 lbs. of bread, 100 lbs. of salted provisions, and 1 gallon of vinegar, but it had not yet gone into effect. Wary of unscrupulous ship agents, owners, and masters, having read von Fürstenwärther's book, and with the Trier municipal sanitarian and medical board examiner, Dr. Willewersch, as his father-in-law, Gall had negotiated a 38-point agreement for safe conditions and sufficient supplies for his emigrants and even presented it to the group for their approval, quite an extraordinary, unprecedented democratic approach.[39]

After a few weeks in Antwerp, they departed on May 25 bound for New York, on the *"Eugénie,"* built for the French navy in Le Havre in 1814, a three-masted vessel based in Brest, France, 92 feet long, 24

---

[37] Gall I, 187-188.

[38] Grabbe, Hans-Jürgen, *Vor der großen Flut: Die europäische Migration in die Vereinigten Staaten von Amerika 1783-1826* (Stuttgart: Steiner, 2001), 125-126.

[39] Gall I, 188.

feet wide, 23 feet deep, 246 tons, coppered and copper plated, naval officers Captain François Jean Allain Jullou, Lieutenant Jules Aimé Conseil, and 2nd Captain Charles Marie Emmanuel Paris, with a crew of 13, newly repurposed as a passenger and cargo ship.[40] They faced the usual hazards–storms (May 29), high waves, calms, icebergs, and fog–and everyday discomforts–seasickness and being stuck in dark, noisy, stifling, stinking, immodest quarters for weeks with people they mostly mistrusted–besides their all being imperiled by a dangerous, nasty, crazed passenger brandishing a knife, who was ultimately chained down. After six weeks on the ocean they caught fresh cod off Newfoundland on July 6, making for a sumptuous breakfast the next morning, their first tangible harbinger of the North American coast.[41]

---

[40] *Les rôles d'équipage de l' «Eugénie»*, held at *Service historique de la Défense*, Brest, France, in *registre 2P7-169, rôle n°41*.

[41] Gall I, 516.

The "Nautilus," Gall, *Meine Auswanderung*, Vol. 1, foldout

The Gall/Tüscher party anchored in New York harbor off Staten Island on July 22 without docking, underwent their medical screening, and stayed offshore for a day and a night. Bullied by tax-shirking New York shipping agents to move on or else be quarantined, they continued on July 24 with the "Nautilus," a steam ferry owned by U.S. Vice-President Daniel D. Tompkins, 126 x 28 ½ feet, with an 8 foot deck height, 70 horsepower, Captain John DeForest, to Perth Amboy, New Jersey. In Perth Amboy they were re-examined by the local Board of Health and pronounced remarkably healthy. There Tüscher's group sold their Swiss timepieces and their bed linens used on the ship. He arranged for a purchase of land on credit and bought oxen, horses, a buggy for the women & infants, and a baggage wagon from Matthias Bruen, a superwealthy business tycoon.[42]

---

[42] Hardesty, H.H., *Hardesty's Historical Hand-Atlas and History of Monroe County, Ohio,* (Chicago: H. H. Hardesty, 1882), 210.

The Proprietary House, courtesy of The Helpful Art Teacher,
Rachel Wintemberg

His mansion, the Proprietary House, now a museum, was built as the residence of colonial New Jersey's royal governor William Franklin, Benjamin Franklin's estranged out-of-wedlock son.[43]

---

[43] www.theproprietaryhouse.org, website accessed June 11, 2016.

Illustration of the Moravian Seminary, Bethlehem, PA, by Illman & Sons

On August 6 the Tüscher party began their overland journey through hospitable Pennsylvania territory. This trip was simultaneously "dusty, exciting, and crowded."[44] Since they could not afford inns, they camped out at night. Their route passed through Easton (where they found two Swiss linen-weavers from the Aargau region), Bethlehem (where the pupils at the co-educational Moravian Seminary provided straw hats, potatoes, bacon, ham, and clothing to the families and sweet treats to the children), Reading (where they ran into Jakob Antenen and other Swiss), Lebanon (on August 19, where they met Jakob Rumpf, a prosperous merchant from Frutigen, Canton Bern), Bedford (where they gave up their worn-out oxen prior to attempting to climb the mountainous Alleghenies and where the local Fankhausers were as wealthy as their entire former village of Trub, the very same Swiss home commune as Niklaus & Daniel Fankhauser and Barbara Baumgartner Tschäppätt of the Tüscher party), Somerset, and Washington, Pennsylvania; and on the National Road just completed in 1819 as far as its new terminus in

---

[44] Irwin, W. B., *The Routes of Migration Between the Atlantic Seaboard and the Midwest*, (Burbank, CA: The Southern California Genealogical Society, 1996), 7.

Wheeling, Virginia (now West Virginia; population 1,567 in 1820). All along their route the young boys begged for food and were generously treated, getting bread with butter or apple butter, meat, cakes, and even money.[45] They felt that they had truly found "a friend in Pennsylvania," as the modern tourism slogan goes. Daniel Fankhauser, Jr., remembering those kindnesses many decades later in 1883, still preferred the Allentown, Pennsylvania, *Welt-Bote* to competing Chicago, Milwaukee, Cincinnati, and New York papers.[46]

On September 15 they left Wheeling to settle downstream on a 5,000-acre tract at the mouth of the Great Kanawha River in Virginia, now West Virginia, which they had agreed to purchase for $3.00 per acre on a 10-year mortgage from Matthias Bruen, one of the richest men in the United States, who owned 200,000 acres there. The land along the Kanawha was in an area where Daniel Boone lived in 1774 and where Cornstalk was defeated, a tract surveyed by and once owned by President George Washington,[47] near where his overseer James Cleveland had made a short-lived outpost in 1775 and by 1776 Cleveland reported that there were 3 dwellings, 11 cabins, and 24 acres planted with corn, potatoes, turnips, and 2,000 peach kernels.[48] Washington's will asserts that "there is no richer, or more valuable land in all that Region."[49] It lies across the Ohio from Gallipolis, Ohio, the home of the "French Five Hundred" settlers, aristocratic misfits in pioneer surroundings, who, like all of our parties of emigrants, fall into the category of unfortunate Europeans who did not wind up owning their anticipated tract of land.

---

[45] Fankhauser, Daniel, Jr., letter in German originally written to *Welt-Bote*, (Allentown, Pennsylvania), July 22, 1883, translated and published by editor G. Tanner as "Traveling of Emigrantes [sic] in 1820" in *Wetzel Independent*, (New Martinsville, WV: The Magnolia Press, October 19, 1933).

[46] Ibid.

[47] www.mountvernon.org/research-collections/maps/the-kanawha-tracts/

[48] Ambler, Charles H., *George Washington and the West*, (Chapel Hill, NC: The University of North Carolina Press, 1936), 156-157.

[49] "Enclosure: Schedule of Property, 9 July 1799," Founders Online, National Archives (http://founders.archives.gov/documents/Washington/06-04-02-0404-0002 [last update: 2016-03-28]). Source: *The Papers of George Washington*, Retirement Series, vol. 4, *20 April 1799–13 December 1799*, ed. W. W. Abbot. Charlottesville: University Press of Virginia, 1999, pp. 512–527.

Illustration of a flatboat by Victor Collot,
from *Voyage dans l'Amerique Septemtrionale*, Paris, 1826

Flatboats obtained at Pittsburgh or Wheeling served as "a combined log cabin, floating barnyard and country store."[50] While coming down the Ohio River the Tüscher flatboat got hung up in low water near Captina (now Powhatan Point) in Belmont County, Ohio, blown during a storm at the end of September, so they had to stop after traveling only 20 miles, unable to continue. Zadock Cramer, the authoritative river guide author, had traveled the area in August 1819, measuring the river level as low as 2.4 feet, and located the sand bar as "a little to the left, just below the foot of [Captina] island."[51] Winter would be coming on before too long, and to get to the Kanawha tract, 103 miles downriver, they would have to walk overland (again) without significant trails or else wade downstream with all their baggage. German-speaking nearby residents George Goetz, a Marylander, and Henry F. Schweppe, later a wholesale grocer and commission merchant in Pittsburgh, advised them that good federal land in the Seven Ranges was worth $2.00 per acre. The hilly topography was reminiscent of their Swiss homeland, with ravines and rock debris of all sizes and shapes, so there they

---

[50] Irwin, 6.
[51] Cramer, Zadock, *The Navigator, Containing Instructions for Navigating the Monongahela, Allegheny, Ohio and Mississippi Rivers: with an Ample Account of These Much Admired Waters, from the Head of the Former to the Mouth of the Latter; and a Concise Description of Their Towns, Villages, Harbors, Settlements, &c.*, (Pittsburgh, PA: Cramer & Spear, 1821), 11th edition, 73, 80.

stayed.[52] Some of the group remained on Captina Creek, but Jakob Tüscher, Bendicht Schneider, and Niklaus Fankhauser settled at Jacob Bare's landing[53] (later Baresville, now Hannibal), in northeastern Monroe County.[54] The three earned 100 pounds of flour and 10 pounds of bacon a day for a short while in October, and Christen Ruegsegger joined them around that time.[55]

---

[52] Arkle, Thomas, Jr., "The Geology of Switzerland Township, Monroe County, Ohio," in *The Ohio Journal of Science*, Vol. LIII, (Columbus, Ohio: The Ohio State University, January, 1953), 1.

[53] Best, Jane Evans, "Bear Saga Update," *Pennsylvania Mennonite Heritage*, (Lancaster, Pennsylvania: Lancaster Mennonite Historical Society, 1988), 22.

[54] An Old Settler, "Reminiscences of Early Days–Settlement of Captina, Belmont County, and Salem and Switzerland Townships, in Monroe County," in *Spirit of Democracy* (Woodsfield, Ohio: Henry R. West, Proprietor, 10 Feb 1874), 2.

[55] Harshbarger, 9.

Niklaus Fankhauser, self-portrait in later years, from Miriam Fankhauser, *The Fankhausers of Monroe County, Ohio*, i

Niklaus Fankhauser was kindly offered a cabin at present-day Sardis in Monroe County by his neighbor Earl Sproat, one of Ohio's original 48 pioneers in 1788, a much younger brother of Sheriff Ebenezer Sproat, the original "Hetuck" (Big Buckeye). In return, carpenter Fankhauser put up fences for him; he fixed up the cabin and two shacks there, harvested some volunteer wheat, planted potatoes, wheat, and hemp, and had enough pasture for his cows. After Fankhauser's house burned down on December 23, 1820, while he was in town buying a spinning wheel, his good neighbors did a house-raising, hastening to help him put up two rudimentary cabins in two days and gave him dressed hogs, flour, clothing, bedding, etc.[56]

Baron von Steiger and his fellow Emigration Commissioner Labarthe of Geneva had contacted U.S, Envoy Extraordinary and Minister Plenipotentiary Albert Gallatin, also a Genevan, in Paris; Gallatin

---

[56] Schelbert, Leo, editor, *America Experienced: Eighteenth and Nineteen Century Accounts of Swiss Immigrants to the United States*, (Camden, Maine: Picton, 1996), 257-258.

warned them that they would experience extreme temperature variations—Russian winters and Spanish summers, he said—in America,[57] and he did not encourage them to emigrate. Undeterred, the first von Steiger transport left Bern on April 26, 1819; others followed a week later. Their trip down the Rhine in a flatboat from Basel to Dordrecht, was stifling, crowded together with their carts, tools, farm implements, household utensils, bedding, seeds, trunks, and crates. The number of emigrants leaving Bern was 123, but one, cabinet-maker Lau, died, slightly more than half dropped out, and some Badeners and Alsatians literally "missed the boat" at the river harbors along the way. The fare quoted in Antwerp for 60 steerage passengers was 9,000 francs, which works out to $28.20 per person, not including food and utensils[58]. His eventual 58 passengers (105 including children) sailed from Antwerp on May 25, 1819, on a Philadelphia-based two-master, the "Columbia," 250 tons, with mahogany-paneled cabins, Captain Daniel L. Kur(t)z, a native of Rheindiebach in the Rhineland, later a citizen of Holland, but naturalized as an American citizen in 1812.[59]

---

[57] von Steiger, Rudolph, letter in German from Federal Creek dated September 1820, in *Der Schweizerfreund*, Year 7, No. 3, "Vaterland: Bern," (Bern: L.A. Haller, Tuesday, January 9, 1821), 1.

[58] Gall I, 201.

[59] "Pennsylvania, Eastern District Naturalization Indexes, 1795-1952," database with images, FamilySearch (https://familysearch.org/ark:/61903/1:1:KXX1-X3Q : 8 December 2014), Daniel L. Kurtz, 1812, citing Naturalization, Pennsylvania, United States, NARA microfilm publication M1248 (Washington D.C.: National Archives and Records administration, n.d.); FHL microfilm 1,412,420.

> NEW YORK, July 10.—*Arr.* schr Mars, Stinman, 19 days from Port au Prince.—*Cl.* ships Grand Seignor, for Gibraltar and a market; Niagara, Bristol, Lisbon; brigs La Bonne Henriette, Jappie, Havre; Mexico, Crowell, Falmouth and a market; Deux Angelique, Joullin, Havre; George Washington, Baker, New Orleans.
> The packet ship Albion, Capt. Williams, sailed this morning for Liverpool.
> *Saturday Evening, July 10.*—Arrived, ship Columbia, Kurtz, of Philadelphia, 47 days from Antwerp, with oil, dry goods, spel'er, &c. and 57 passengers. *Left*, May 25th, ship Bramin, of Boston, for the Baltic, in three weeks; ship Maria, Bates, of Boston, uncertain; a ship under Prussian colors taking in passengers for New York; and a French ship for do. with passengers. July 8th, lat 34, 56, long 76, 30, *spoke* the schr Haley, or Hulsey, of Thomastown, from Boston for Alexandria.

Boston Daily Advertiser, 14 Jul 1819

The "Columbia" transported oil, cocoa, alum, 360 muskets, 1,450 pair of pistols, [60] slates, furs, dry goods, spelter,[61] sail duck, Madeira and Tenerife wine, toys, pictures, etc., consigned to F. & A. Brunell, McCrea & Slidell, B. Grauer, J. Gonen, P. Beatnell, Taylor & Wilder, M. Durand, GG & S Howland, C. Schoulstew, J. Diamond of Philadelphia, Montgomery & Sons of Philadelphia, Warden & Brothers of Philadelphia, and I. Kugler.[62] After weeks on the Atlantic, they spotted numerous whales along the Newfoundland banks and fished for shark and cod for two days.

They reached New York on July 10, cheerfully described as "industrious Swiss, who had forsaken their mountains and valleys, their lakes and glaciers, to breathe more freely the air of liberty in the new world; the men in 'russet mantle clad,' with mild looks and sun burnt complexions; the women, with tight bodices, short petticoats, and hair in long and graceful plaits, holding their ruddy

---

[60] *Mercantile Advertiser* (New York, NY, Wednesday, 14 Jul 1819, issue 8000), 2.
[61] *Evening Post* (New York, NY, Monday, 13 Jul 1819, issue 5235), 2.
[62] "Marine News," *New York Gazette* (New York, NY, Monday, July 12, 1819, Vol. XXIX, issue 11707), 2.

children by the hand."[63] They later continued to Philadelphia, arriving on August 2 to 98° weather and in the midst of a yellow fever scare; that epidemic eventually moved north, where it claimed Dr. DeWitt, the New York Health Officer, on September 11, 1819, at the Quarantine.[64]

Originally intending to go west to the Red River or perhaps Indiana, which already had a Swiss wine colony, the Baron's caravan, with the von Steigers riding in their small Bernese coach, the women and children riding, and the men walking, headed across the Alleghenies with eight huge Conestoga wagons (mostly containing the Baron's personal baggage) from Philadelphia via Downingtown, Lancaster, Harrisburg, Chambersburg, Bedford, and Pittsburgh, Pennsylvania.[65]

---

[63] Howard, first name not given, in *The National Advocate*, (New York, NY, Saturday, July 31, 1819).

[64] Townsend, Peter S., M.D., *An Account of the Yellow Fever As It Prevailed in the City of New-York, in the Summer and Autumn of 1822*, (New York: O. Halsted, 1823), 373.

[65] Lehmann, Mary Jean (Johnson), *The Family of Daniel Uhl II (1768-1853) and Wilhelmina de Steiguer Uhl (1802-1853)*, 129.

Illustration from Rudolf Cronau, *Drei Jahrhunderte deutschen Lebens in Amerika*, Berlin, 1909, 256

The families went down the Ohio River on a 60 x 14 foot flatboat with cabins, purchased in Pittsburgh, possibly poled by John Finsterwald, orphaned son of a Swiss boatman, who grew up in Stilli, a town full of boatmen. Glancing at a map, Switzerland is seemingly a landlocked country, but there are many mountain lakes, including Lake Geneva, Lake Lucerne, Lake Neuchatel, Lake Thun, and Lake Zurich, where most of the major Swiss cities arose, and rivers such as the Aare (where Stilli is located) and the Rhine. In any case Finsterwald, as the son of a boatman, was dubbed the "Captain." The many things the Swiss had to contend with on the Ohio included narrow channels, shifting sandbars, rocks, snags, and islands emerging in the stream through the extreme low water during the summer of 1819. After their lengthy ocean and overland journey, the party took the occasion for a traditional Swiss break to wash and dry their clothes beside the river. [66] It was the custom that "in Switzerland clothes were washed only twice a year, in spring and

---

[66] Byers, Samuel Hawkins Marshall, *Switzerland and the Swiss*, (Zurich: Orell Füssli, 1875), 92.

autumn."[67] That Ohio River cleaning included the Baron's copious supply of 44 dozen [sic!] fine white linen shirts.[68] They were laid up at Mile Run just a mile downstream from Marietta, Ohio, where they had run aground on a sandbar in shallow water. Zadock Cramer had sounded the depth at this point in August as low as 2.6 feet.[69] At Marietta, Baron von Steiger's personal physician sued him because he had been ordered to do menial labor working jack screws and levers to free the flatboat. For the trial, David Uhl, who would become the Baron's future son-in-law, was called in by the authorities to interpret English to German and vice versa.[70]

On October 19 in Marietta the Baron was induced to buy land. By wining and dining the Baron, land agent Benjamin Pitt Putnam and his father David Putnam, great-grandson and grandson respectively of General Israel Putnam ("Old Put" of the Battle of Bunker Hill), persuaded him to purchase 3,840 uncleared acres owned by Levi Barber, a surveyor, member of Congress, and land office receiver, and Paul Fearing, a Northwest Territory legislator, the first lawyer in Ohio. The 3,200 acres bought from Barber were contiguous 640-acre lots from the five Ohio Company shares once owned by the heirs of John Paul Jones as compensation for his service.[71] The tract was located along Federal Creek in Ames and Canaan Townships in Athens County, where the Baron would build his *Steigersruh*, Steiger's Repose, the center of his new Switzerland.

---

[67] Jewett, Ruth (Harbecke), "The Story of Emilie Joss-Bigler," *Newsletter, Swiss American Historical Society,* Vol. XXI, No. 3, (Norfolk, VA: Old Dominion University, November 1985), 11.

[68] Lehmann, Mary Jean (Johnson), *The Family of Daniel Uhl ...,* 129.

[69] Cramer, 79, 80.

[70] de Steiguer (1888), 24.

[71] Hoskins, 152.

Illustration from Rudolf Cronau, *Drei Jahrhunderte deutschen Lebens in Amerika*, Berlin, 1909, 267

The Steiger/Stalder party's women and children stayed at Marietta while the menfolk went ahead to build a substantial two-story log house for the Baron and, later, small cabins for their families. They sold their flatboat in October and purchased hogs, cattle, etc., at Belpre, Washington County,[72] across from the historic Blennerhassett Island. That "enchanted isle" is where Harman Blennerhassett, another European nobleman in an off-limits marriage, had settled in 1798 and built his since-burned Palladian mansion, where Aaron Burr had promoted his colony in the Southwest in 1805 and 1806. Now the women and children followed the men on foot through the untamed bush to their new locale, where they had to camp out at first.[73] Their four-footed neighbors included deer, bears, red and gray foxes, bobcats, and nightly howling wolves, and besides those, there were snakes (some of them poisonous rattlers), but the Baron was gratified to find God-fearing

---

[72] "Die schweizerischen Auswanderungen der vier letzten Jahrhunderte, Bechluß," in *Morgenblatt für gebildete Stände*, No. 91, Tuesday, April 16, 1822, 361-362.

[73] de Steiguer (1888), 25.

and friendly farmers living nearby.[74] During bad weather that first winter everybody gathered together at the Baron's lodge, which had a fine warm fireplace. The Baron later reported to his friends in Switzerland that all his "Columbia" passengers were healthy throughout, like those on the "*Eugénie.*" They also had sufficient provisions as contracted by Gall and ordered by Baron von Steiger.

A five-state joint Ohio River Commission had been appointed to study the obstructions to navigation, consisting of John Adair, soon-to-be Governor of Kentucky; Senator Walter Lowrie from Pennsylvania; General Samuel Blackburn, a Virginia legislator; and General Edward White Tupper, a surveyor and ship & gunboat builder of Marietta, the Ohio commissioner. In their report dated November 2 the commission, utilizing the expertise of surveyor Magnus Miller Murray, an accomplished Renaissance man who later became the Mayor of Pittsburgh, mapped 102 impediments in the Ohio River between Pittsburgh and Louisville in 1819.[75] Many sandbanks had built up at the mouths of streams flowing into the slow-moving Ohio River where wash of gravel, sand, and silt from steep hillsides had gradually accumulated, forming the two fateful sandbars at Little Captina Creek and Mile Run.[76]

Two other Swiss colonization commissioners, Samuel Reichenbach from Bern, who drafted the printed plan for the colony,[77] with his son, and Jean Joseph Labarthe from Geneva, bringing his family, traveled with the Baron on the "Columbia." On August 13 in Philadelphia a panel of three Philadelphia arbitrators, 1) Louis Krumbhaar (a well-connected Leipzig-born pharmaceutical importer

---

[74] von Steiger, Rudolph, Extract of a letter in German begun in August 1819 and concluded on January 13, 1820, from Federal Creek, State of Ohio in North America, in *Nachblatt zum Schweizerfreund,* No. 14, (Bern: L. A. Haller, April 7, 1820), 171-172.

[75] Frost, Sherman L., and Walter Mitsch, "Resource Development and Conservation History Along the Ohio River," (Columbus, Ohio: The Ohio State University, 1989), in *Ohio Journal of Science,* 89 (5), 145.

[76] E-mail to the author from professional geologist Don Gardner, Reno, Ohio, November 18, 2015.

[77] *Aarauer Zeitung,* Aarau, Switzerland, 1819, 221.

who in 1832 would escort Prince Maximilian of Wied-Neuwied through Philadelphia), 2) Charles von Bonnhorst (a German-born merchant and banker, later postmaster of Pittsburgh), and 3) Henry J. Williams (an attorney, who in 1820 would marry Julia, daughter of Dr. Benjamin Rush, first chemistry professor in the U.S., medical educator, abolitionist, and signer of the Declaration of Independence), ruled that Reichenbach and Labarthe owed Ludwig Gall 1,081 francs plus 1,552 francs to reimburse Gall for advance payments he had made.[78] Krumbhaar and Williams decided in favor of Gall after Gall produced a receipt proving his payment. Displeased, Reichenbach and Labarthe parted company with Gall.

Pursuing his own fortune, notary Samuel Reichenbach landed at Arkansas Post, capital of Arkansas Territory, in June 1820, looking to purchase land in Winter's Grant. Reichenbach planned to form his own colony along the Arkansas River for between 100 and 1,000 Swiss settlers,[79] but that never materialized; reportedly he considered returning to Europe, but died of yellow fever.[80]

The Reformed French-speaking Genevan trader Jean Joseph Labarthe gravitated to Louisiana with his family. Labarthe's children assimilated in Catholic Louisiana; they became traders in New Orleans, planters and a physician in Assumption Parish, and a riverboat captain on the Mississippi River whose steamboat was seized without compensation during the Civil War and who was reduced to selling dried Spanish moss in his old age. Some descendants still live in Louisiana.

As for Ludwig Gall, he and his young wife Maria Anna Willewersch, as well as his parents and his little dog, traveled in cabin accommodations on the "*Eugénie.*" While waiting for his Switzers to

---

[78] Gall I, 351-357.
[79] *Arkansas Weekly Gazette,* Little Rock, AR, Saturday, June 17, 1820, Vol. 1, Issue 31, 3.
[80] Howard, Arnold, letter dated January 30, 1825, from Pittsburgh, in Leo Schelbert and Hedwig Rappolt, *Alles ist ganz anders hier: Auswandererschicksale in Briefen aus zwei Jahrhunderten* (Zurich: Limmat, 1984), 201

arrive in Antwerp, Gall had gotten into a disagreement with some Separatist leaders of a group of 385 settlers recruited from Württemberg who possibly intended to join Josephsurname Bimeler's two-year-old Separatist community at Zoar, Tuscarawas County, Ohio, or Georg Rapp's *Harmonie Gesellschaft* (Harmony Society) at New Harmony, Posey County, Indiana, on the Wabash River. They were going to travel on the "Admittance," Captain McLaughlin, 238 tons, 142 passengers, and the "Emma," Captain Ritzrow, 299 tons, carrying linens, brass, and 248 passengers. In fact, the "Admittance" and "Emma" were already overbooked beyond the limits of Pennsylvania's 1818 Health Law, and the "Emma" was lacking a *Türkenpass*, a Mediterranean safe passage. Nevertheless, Gall was anonymously given false information disparaging the "*Eugénie*" to try to trick him into joining their party. It was a good thing that Gall did not fall for this swindle of the two-faced Captain Ritzrow. Beyond the unconscionable overcrowding, the Separatists were charged more per person for their passage than Gall was, and even so, in Philadelphia Captain Ritzrow sued to be paid again. The double-dealer knew full well that he had never issued them a written receipt; the reprehensible captain even succeeded in sending five of the twelve Separatist leaders into debtor's prison, namely J.G. Albrecht, C. Laich [Baisch?], C. [Johann Christoph] Platz, and U. [Johann Ulrich?] Mayer. Another leader, Jacob Witzmann/Wizemann, from Frommern, Württemberg, had fallen into the Delaware River and drowned while disembarking.[81]

Although hunger was still widespread in Switzerland, the food in the port city was more available and better-tasting fare. In Antwerp Gall's party stayed at the *Pot d'Etain* ("Tin Pot") boarding house, where at a typical meal (here, on April 27) each table could choose their menu home-style from pots of hearty beef soup, beans, calf ribs, boiled potatoes, seafood, juicy roast beef, lobster, roasting chickens, lettuce salad, and beer.[82]

---

[81] Gall I, 134.
[82] Gall I, 101.

Witmer's Tavern, photo by Jeanne Ruzchak-Eckman

After arriving in New York, the Gall family traveled to Perth Amboy, New Jersey, on the "Nautilus," from there to New Brunswick with the "Bellona," 116 tons, with a copper engine, designed and piloted by Captain Cornelius Vanderbilt, the future shipping and railroad tycoon and founder of Vanderbilt University;[83] from there on the "Rambler" to Princeton, Bordentown, where Gall visited Napoleon's elder brother Joseph Bonaparte, Count Sürvilliers, the ex-King of Naples, Sicily, and Spain, now residing in his "Point Breeze" estate, well-liked by his neighbors,[84] from there by post chaises (stagecoaches) overland to Trenton, then on August 2 via the "Aetna" owned by Bonaparte/Sürvilliers, down the Delaware River to Philadelphia.[85] Gall's caravan stayed at notable Pennsylvania inns, most of them now on the National Register of Historic Places: the Black Horse Inn (=Sampson and the Lion) in Flourtown on August 19, the General Washington Inn in Downingtown on August 20,[86] the

---

[83] Gall II, 32-33.
[84] Gall II, 83.
[85] Gall II, 92.
[86] Gall II, 180.

Conestoga Inn (=Witmer's Tavern) on August 21 and 22, and in Lancaster on August 23.[87]

The indentured servants whose passages Gall had prepaid surreptitiously dropped out along the way, some pilfering Gall's property, vanishing into the local communities (including Johann Mollenkopf of Pfullingen, Andreas Jung of Retzefeld (Ritzenfeld?), and Joseph Cornet of Antwerp, in New Jersey; Daniel Houbar of Liége and Christian Liebeskind of Weimar, in Philadelphia; Nicolaus Eberhart, Heinrich Kuhl, Philipp Biehl, and Theodor Heit, all of Marburg, and a Swiss named Johann Machern, at Downingtown; and Peter Wissel of Mömbris-Rappach, at Harrisburg)[88] at a time when the Redemptioner system was dying and when the servants had seen American-style freedom firsthand. An English traveler of the era observed that "a common mode of resenting an imperious order, is to quit the house, without waiting or even asking for a reckoning."[89] Evidently the Europeans had quickly taken to liberated American ways.

On an excursion, Gall reconnoitered Cincinnati and the Miami Valley as potential settlement sites and formulated a plan to create a *Deutschheim*, "a German city, which was to become the nucleus of further German penetration."[90] However, he returned to Pennsylvania's fledgling capital city, where he had rented a villa with 36 acres. There he founded a Colonization Society of Harrisburg for a settlement in northwestern Pennsylvania, hoping to draw extensive landholders in the most German U.S. state, "as well calculated for the interest of the owners as for the benefit of the settlers,"[91] but in a terrible economy with money scarce, few were able to invest. Gall

---

[87] Gall II, 183.
[88] Grabbe, 382.
[89] Wright, 461.
[90] von Senger und Etterlin, Stefan, "New Germany in North America: Origins, Processes, and Responses, 1815-1860," in *Emigration and Settlement Patterns of German Communities in North America*, (Indianapolis, IN: Max Kade German-American Center, 1995), 151.
[91] *Free Press*, Lancaster, Pennsylvania, November 2, 1820, Volume II, Issue 26, 1.

called his Harrisburg villa "*Bellevue*," featuring mahogany and faux marble wall finishing[92] by his accompanying painter Louis Auguste Decaen, with furnishings bought in Philadelphia and imported from Europe, a piano, and a billiards table.[93] He and his father pursued the family trade by purveying wines and liqueurs from Europe.

But to be a new foreign arrival selling imports in the poor economy of 1819 and 1820 in a city of only 2,990 population, now without his redemptioner help, and situated on the frontier where the locals can distill plenty of home-grown whiskey out of corn, was not the right time nor place nor situation. Mary Sarah Bilder succinctly sums up Gall's predicament during that fateful time: "With economic collapse, 1819 had brought the end of indentured servitude. With the new act [i.e. the Steerage Act], 1819 brought the beginning of a new institution: 'immigration.'"[94] The Galls decided to go back home to Trier in October 1820. To top off their distress, on the return journey to Europe their ship sprang a leak in the English Channel while approaching Dover, a suitable metaphor for the plummeting fortune of Gall's American adventure. They required a cutter to come rescue them and take them the remaining ten hours to shore.

---

[92] *Der deutsche Pionier*, Cincinnati, Vol. 13, 1881, Heft 2, 47-49.

[93] *Notes and Queries Historical and Genealogical Chiefly Relating to Interior Pennsylvania*, edited by William Henry Egle, reprint first and second series, Volume II, 108.

[94] Bilder, Mary Sarah, "The Struggle over Immigration: Indentured Servants, Slaves, and Articles of Commerce," *Missouri Law Review*, (Columbia, MO: University of Missouri, 1996), Vol. 61, Issue 4, Fall 1996, Article 1, 792. Available at: http://scholarship.law.missouri.edu/mlr/vol61/iss4/1

Their Circumstances

Chorgerichtsmanual, Canton Bern, judgment sentencing Jakob and Katharina to prison, 28 March 1816, 131.

Jakob Tüscher was expelled from Switzerland. He had repeatedly been chastised by the *Chorgericht* in Bern, a powerful ecclesiastical marriage and morals tribunal for family, church, and school that would be abolished in 1832.[95] A Swiss genealogist, Yvonne Gygli, theorized that "they may have been *Wiedertäufer*, or Anabaptists," and the established Protestant church simply did not recognize the marriage.[96] Swiss-American historian John Paul von Grüningen claimed: "The townships of Switzerland and Ohio in Monroe County were settled as early as 1819 by Bernese Mennonites."[97]

---

[95] Letter to the author from Dr. Fritz Stalder of Bern on January 17, 1989.
[96] Tisher, Lester John, *The Strange Story of Jacob Tisher*, (Bremerton, Washington: self-published, 2000), 2.
[97] von Grüningen, John Paul, *The Swiss in the United States,* (Madison, Wisconsin: Swiss-American Historical Society, 1940), 21.

Most Swiss dissenters conformed to the Reformed Church rules as necessary. In Bern there were 277,100 Protestants, 42,000 Catholics (in the area of the former Bishopric of Basel), the two established state churches, but only about 900 open Anabaptists in 1819.[98] Though there were two earlier Mennonites in Ernst Müller's *Geschichte der Bernischen Täufer* named Jacob Marti, the same as a member of Tüscher's party, and his daughter-in-law was a Marti, the Tüscher surname was not listed there, nor was it in Delbert Gratz's *Bernese Anabaptists*.[99] The two files on Jakob Tüscher in the Bernese State Archives failed to disclose any overt Anabaptist connection.[100]

By Bernese law all Swiss were required to register vital events with the omnipresent Swiss Reformed church (or Catholic in the Basel diocese area); legitimacy had to be established through baptism and marriages officiated by an establishment church pastor. Neither of Tüscher's overlapping relationships with Elisabetha Arn and Katharina Winterberger was solemnized by a minister of the Swiss Reformed church. Marriage to a partner who had produced extramarital children was prohibited. This injunction would explain why the births of all of Tüscher's children except Abraham were considered out of wedlock, and yet the morals court paradoxically would *"absolute verbieten"* (absolutely forbid) him to marry their mother.[101] In 1819 the patriarch and his entire family of exiles were gladly granted permission to leave Canton Bern, for fear that the local government would support his large clan indefinitely. The condition for Tüscher's reprieve set by the Bernese lower council to the court in Fraubrunnen on March 16, 1819, was his agreeing to the banishment of his family; the surety was that their cash and travel documents would be confiscated until they were in a European port on board a ship.[102]

---

[98] Meyer, Ludwig Gerold, *Abriß der Erdbeschreibung und Staatskunde der Schweiz* (Zürich: Füeßli und Comp., 1824), 132.

[99] Email to the author from Cristian Consuegra, March 8, 2017.

[100] Ibid.

[101] *Manual des Chorgerichts der Stadt und Republik Bern*, (Bern, Switzerland: March 28, 1816), 131.

[102] May, Rudolf, "Schreiben des Kleinen Rates an den Oberamtmann von Fraubrunnen," March 22, 1819, Dokument 4, *Berner Zeitschrift für Geschichte und Heimatkunde,* Vol. 50, 74-75.

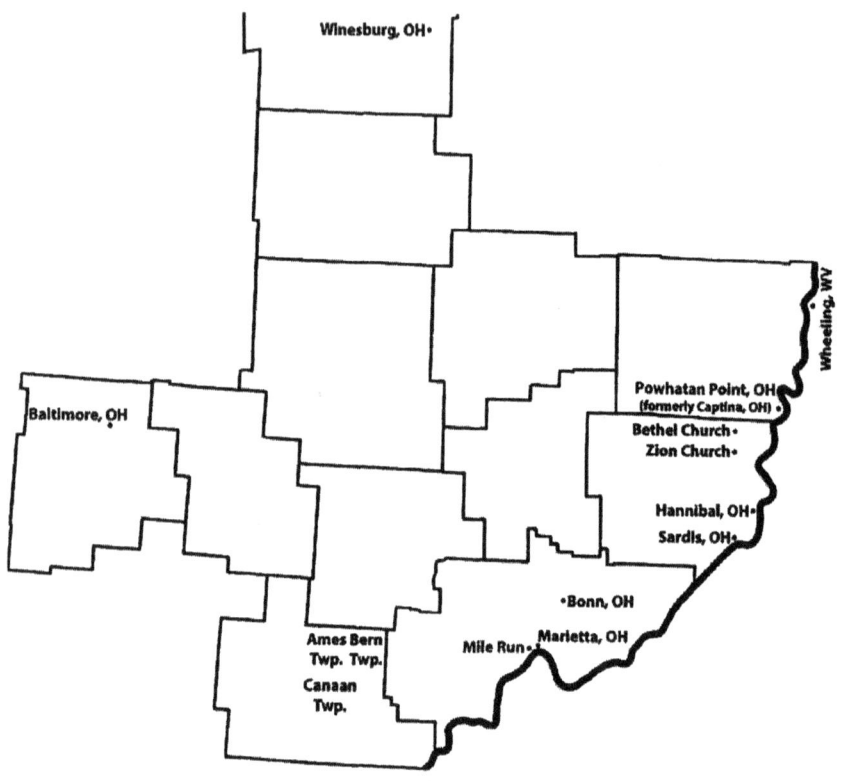

Swiss settlements in southeastern Ohio.
Graphic: Andrea Adkins, Washington County Public Library

Tisher's party burned their bridges behind them for a more tolerant land. In Ohio, Jacob Tisher became engaged in a vocation of faith. "Father Tisher" was in the forefront of evangelistic German Methodism. He taught a German Sabbath school in his home as early as 1825, attracting scholars from five and six miles around, and preached in English at homes in his neighborhood by 1835.[103] He was known to and possibly converted by the earlier Methodist missionary Adam Miller, a Maryland-born former Mennonite who spoke Pennsylvania German (basically an eastern Palatine dialect, spoken by Swiss settlers who repopulated that area after the Thirty Years' War) and who was active along the Ohio River in southeastern

---

[103] *Spirit of Democracy*, February 10, 1874, 2.

Ohio.[104] In 1839 and 1840 Tisher was encouraged to continue by three pillars of the church, none other than the founder of German Methodism, Wilhelm Nast of Cincinnati, born in Stuttgart, and editor of *Der Christliche Apologete*, "an excellently edited newspaper intended ... for the entire German-American community"[105]; John Zwahlen/Swahlen of Schwarzenburg, Canton Bern, born on Christmas Day 1808 and baptized on New Year's Day 1809 in Wahlern, Canton Bern, of Wheeling, Virginia (now West Virginia), later a missionary in Zürich; and Engelhardt Riemenschneider, minister of various churches in the Ohio Valley, later a Methodist missionary in Friedrichsdorf in his native Hessen.[106] Nast visited Tisher's congregants in Switzerland Township on March 18 and 19, 1840, on his way to dedicate the first German Methodist edifice built in the world in Wheeling, Virginia (now West Virginia), on March 22 and 23.[107]

---

[104] Miller, Adam, *Experience of German Methodist Preachers*, (Cincinnati: Methodist Book Concern, 1859), 59-63.
[105] Tolzmann, Don Heinrich, *Cincinnati's German Heritage*, (Bowie, MD: Heritage Books, Inc., 1994), 58.
[106] Tüscher, Jakob. Letter in German from the Monroe [Methodist] Mission to Wilhelm Nast dated February 9, 1840, published in "Mittheilungen aus dem Reich Christi," *Der christliche Apologete*," March 13, 1840, 3, cols. 2-3.
[107] *Der christliche Apologete*, March 13, 1840, 3, col. 5, and *Western Christian Advocate*, March 13, 1840, Vol. 6, 47.

Illustration from *The Circuit Rider* by Edward Eggleston, 1887.

Aquatint by Jacques Milbert, "American Methodists proceeding to their Camp Meeting," 1819

"Father Tisher" was a local preacher and subsequently an itinerant missionary of the Monroe Mission of the Pittsburgh Conference. His 200-mile circuit covered a three-county area 40 miles wide by 70 miles long,[108] which he covered every four weeks, mostly on foot, partially by steamboat, and locally on horseback.[109]

Jim Baker cartoon, *The Ohio Adventure,* May 15, 1968

Along his path in rough, hilly, unimproved southeastern Ohio, he helped plant German-speaking Methodist churches in Marietta and Bonn, Washington County, and two that he named Bethel (Hebrew

---

[108] Miller, Adam, *Origin and Progress of the German Missions in the Methodist Episcopal Church, Including an Account of the Christian Experience of Some of the Converts from Popery and Infidelity, As Furnished by Themselves,* (Cincinnati, OH: J. P. Wright and L. Swormstedt for the Methodist Episcopal Church, 1843), 88-89.

[109] Tisher, Charles Daniel, and Grace F. Schafer, *Tisher Family Came to America from Switzerland 1819,* (Salt Lake City, Utah: self-published, 1979), 3.

for "house of God"), 6 miles from Clarington,[110] and Zion (Israel, a "new Jerusalem," an ideal community of believers) on Cain Ridge in Salem Township[111] in the secluded hills of Monroe County, in his Monroe Mission, along with Carl C. (Charles Carroll) Best, a first-generation German-American.[112] Tisher wrote a letter in German to the *Amerikanische Missionsgesellschaft* (American Mission Society), denouncing those he viewed as false preachers and deploring an overall moral corruption among the influx of settlers, a copy of which he sent to all those he condemned.[113]

The Monroe and Belmont County Swiss settlement attracted additional Switzers and also Germans, and the Swiss travel guide author Adolf Ott described it (as well as Stark and Tuscarawas Counties) as a new "*Kanton Bern.*"[114] The humble folks here were content to mind their own business and live simple lives in a geographically remote area, apart from a materialistic world. As the hundredth anniversary booklet of St. John's (Evangelical, later United Church of Christ) in Powhatan Point, Belmont County, puts it: "Determined to make good, they built their little log cabins, a task not without difficulties, and then undertook the herculean task of clearing the timber-covered hills, to procure ground for cultivation. Their aim, however, was not merely to gain material, but also

---

[110] Dixon, Barbara, *A Forgotten Heritage: The German Methodist Church*, (Milford, OH: Little Miami Publishing Co., 2011), 334-335.

[111] Dixon, 335-337.

[112] Golder, C[hristian], John H. Horst, and J[ohn] G[eorge] Schaal, editors, *Geschichte der Zentral Deutschen Konferenz Einschließlich der Anfangsgeschichte des deutschen Methodismus*, (Cincinnati: Jennings & Graham, 1907), 27.

[113] Tüscher, Jakob, letter written March 12, 1834 to *Amerikanische Missionsgesellschaft* (the American Mission Society), which he sent in multiple copies to churches and individuals mentioned in his letter, original in possession of William I. Tisher of Rittman, Ohio, in 1987.

[114] Ott, Adolf, *Der Führer nach Amerika für Reisebegleiter und geographisches Handbuch enthaltend Schilderungen über die Ver. Staaten von Amerika, Canada, Argentinien, Chile, Uruguay, Paraguay und Südbrasilien unter steter Berücksichtigung der wirthschaftliche Verhältnisse sowie der Kolonisation*, (Basel: Felix Schneider/Adolf Geering, 1882), 330-331.

spiritual wealth."[115] Religions were free to evangelize in this rich soil, and "the good seed of the Word did not fall upon stony ground."[116]

Methodist minister and later missionary Engelhardt Riemenschneider wrote that in these hills, inhabited mostly by Swiss and Alsatians, there was a "hunger for the Word of God" in 1839. People came from seven miles away over unimproved roads. Even after a two-foot snowfall, he reports that almost nobody was absent from church.[117] Jakob Baumberger, previously resident in Obersteckholz, Canton Bern, formerly a preacher for 14 years at the *Evangelische Gesellschaft* in Bern, became a popular minister of the aforementioned St. John's church in Powhatan Point, as well as other Swiss congregations in Holmes and Monroe Counties, between his immigration in 1850 and his death in 1854.[118] As late as 1906 Pastor Theodore Rudin, born in Bubendorf, Canton Basel-Landschaft, was amazed when he arrived at his new assignment in Powhatan Point to be greeted by parishioners with a *"Grüezi"* or "God greet you"[119] in his familiar native *Schwyzertüütsch* vernacular.[120]

In this burgeoning field ripe for more Swiss newcomers near Sardis in Monroe County, the community became the home of the second Apostolic Christian Church in the U.S. where, as history repeated

---

[115] *Booklet for The One Hundredth Anniversary of St. John's Evangelical Congregation, Powhatan Point, Ohio, H. G. Schuessler, Pastor, Observed the 11th and 12th Days of June, 1927,* (Powhatan Point, OH: St. John's Evangelical Church, 1927), 5.

[116] *Booklet.*, 5.

[117] Tolzmann, Don Heinrich, *Engelhardt Riemenschneider: Memoirs of a German Methodist Pioneer,* translated by Edwin A. Riemenschneider, (Milford, OH: Little Miami Publishing Co., 2015), 45.

[118] Obituary for Johann Jacob Baumberger in *Der Friedensbote,* official newspaper of the *Evangelischer Kirchenverein des Westens,* Vol. 6, No. 1 (January 1, 1855), 13.

[119] An Old Settler, "Reminiscences...," 2.

[120] Romick, Karen, *Our German-Speaking Heritage,* speech text (Monroe County Chapter of Ohio Genealogical Society: Woodsfield, Ohio, April 21, 2002). http://freepages.history.rootsweb.ancestry.com/~harringtonfamilies/German-speaking.htm, accessed June 13, 2016.

itself, a flatboat of Swiss ran aground at Duffy Run, Duffy, Ohio, perhaps, as a church historian put it, "as a sign of God's leading" them to a place located just down the hill from the current church.[121] This occurred during the late summer Ohio River low water of 1848, the same season when 60 steamboats became stranded at Cincinnati, unable to proceed downstream.[122] The church was established by Isaac Gehring of Buchberg, Canton Schaffhausen, who married Margaretha Maibach of Dürrenroth, Canton Bern, and Bendicht Weyeneth of Lüterkofen, Canton Solothurn, born in Lüsslingen, Canton Solothurn, who married Elisabeth Blunier, who was born on 26 Apr 1824 "in der Neumatt" at Trub, Canton Bern; these founders called it their "New Zion." Gehring and Weyeneth were influenced by Samuel Heinrich Fröhlich, born 4 Jul 1803 in Brugg, Canton Aargau, founder of the *Neutäufer* (Swiss Baptist) movement in the Emmental region. Some of the earliest Monroe County members were the Aeschlimann, Gehring, and Gerber families.[123]

Local place and organization names reveal the indelible Swiss history. Monroe County has its Switzerland Township, which split off from Salem Township in 1827 when Johannes Keller's mattock, his livelihood, was seized by the tax assessor, and his fellow Swiss also balked in protest.[124] Today the high school vocational students attend Swiss Hills Career Center, which serves the entire Switzerland of Ohio Local School District. A local 4-H club is the Hilltop Swiss Lads and Lassies. Former post offices in Monroe County were called Dairy, a communal cheese-making site, and Switzer. Rural historian Otto Brunner, teacher and director at the Strickhof agricultural

---

[121] Klopfenstein, Perry A., *Marching to Zion: A History of the Apostolic Christian Church of America 1847-2007*, Second Edition, (Fort Scott, KS: The Apostolic Christian Church of America, 2008), 30.

[122] http://www.ohiomemory.org/cdm/ref/collection/p267401coll36/id/4168, multi-daguerreotype panoramic photograph of Cincinnati taken from Newport, Kentucky, on September 24, 1848 by William S. Porter and Charles Fontayne (Cincinnati, Ohio: Public Library of Cincinnati & Hamilton County, digitally restored 2011).

[123] Klopfenstein, 29.

[124] Maienknecht, Theresa A., and Maienknecht, Stanley B., *Monroe County, Ohio: A History*, (Clarksville, Ohio: Windmill Publications, 1989), Chapter XXX, "Switzerland Township," 409.

institute in Canton Zürich, Switzerland, and a consultant in West Virginia, recorded that in 1877 this little-known settlement produced an astounding 199,475 pounds of cheese, 45,185 pounds of butter, and 2,486 gallons of wine, all typical Swiss products.[125] In 1927 there were still six remaining cheese producers in Switzer and two in Clarington who advertised in a local church commemorative booklet.[126] Abel's Cheese in Sardis and the Witschey chain of markets and Swiss Valley Associates are current businesses in 2017 that remind us of the heritage.

---

[125] Brunner, Otto, *Die Auswanderung nach den Vereinigten Staaten: amerikanische landwirthschaftliche Verhältnisse und ein neues Ansiedlungs-Projekt,* (Bern: Kommissions-Verlag von Huber & Cie., 1881), 33.
[126] *Booklet,* unpaginated advertising section.

Coat of Arms of the (black ibex) von Steiger de Granson Family, *Berner Wappenbuch*, 1932

Baron von Steiger had to leave Switzerland because his romances had made him an outcast in Swiss society, shunned by his own patrician family. They strongly disapproved of his marriage to a commoner, subsequent divorce, and affair with another commoner, his miller's daughter. Napoleon had dismantled the Swiss social order with the anti-nobility concept of *égalité*, stripping Bernese Chief Magistrate Niklaus Friedrich von Steiger of his office in 1798 and forcibly imposing the Helvetic Republic (1798-1803). Baron Johann Rudolf von Steiger was captured by the French and imprisoned for 18 months, creating his intense lifelong hatred for Napoleon. But because of his peccadillos he found himself in an unsustainable position in Europe (we already know about the strict Bernese marriage laws). Among the von Steigers with a black ibex in the coat of arms he would surely be considered the "black sheep" of the family.

The Baron was a proud man, so to save face he represented himself as a patriotic Swiss colonizer establishing a miniature Switzerland on a new continent. He was "imperious, strong-minded, and strong-willed," accustomed to having his orders obeyed without question, but once in the New World his status as hereditary nobility and a military officer in Europe meant nothing outside his circle. The U.S. Constitution forbids noble titles, and independent-minded Americans disregarded his authority. When he tried to flaunt his rank in a confrontation with Gall at the harbor in Philadelphia, he was deflated. Even a fellow aristocrat, the America commentator Baron Moritz von Fürstenwärther, who was at the harbor with Gall, set Steiger straight about social equality in America.[127] This new mindset forced a drastic readjustment for the Baron. Yet at heart Steiger was said to be "particularly sympathetic and unsuspecting toward his friends and those whom he found in distress."[128]

Settled in his Ohio home in 1820, evoking his traditional church background, the Baron wrote that on Sundays he read aloud Swiss Reformed sermons published by a popular preacher, David Müslin of the *Münster* (Cathedral) in Bern, and his settlers were singing hymns and psalms from their familiar hymnals and psalters they had brought with them. In 1824, though, he introduced the Swedenborgian or New Jerusalem religion into the area in the person of Chaplain Daniel Thune/Thuun,[129] a merchant whom he had met in Philadelphia. The Baron built a brick chapel for Thune, with its front steps carved into a sandstone bank.[130] 21 members of his settlement signed a statement "heartily endorsing" the New Jerusalem doctrine.[131] The Baron sent his namesake son, Rodolphe de Steiguer, Jr., to Henderson, New York, to study to become a Swedenborgian minister, but young Rodolphe bypassed his father's wishes and wound up marrying Laura Watson Ames, the sister of

---

[127] Gall I, 349.

[128] de Steiguer (1888), 156

[129] Steinach, Adelrich, *Geschichte und Leben der Schweizer Kolonien in den Vereinigten Staaten unter Mitwirkung des amerikanischen Grütlibundes*, 220-221.

[130] Steinach, Adelrich, editor, *Swiss Colonists in 19th Century America*, with new introduction in English and indexes by Urspeter Schelbert, (Camden, Maine: Picton, 1995 (1889)).

[131] "Annals of the New-Church in America, 1824-1829," *The New-Church Magazine*, (Boston, Massachusetts: Massachusetts New-Church Union, 1873), Vol. 1, 30-31.

future Methodist Bishop Edward Ames, and he later became a member of the Cumberland Presbyterian Church in Athens.

The former Baron, handsome, an imposing 6'2"[132] and well-framed,[133] wearing a wig and glasses,[134] was the master of the household at his 585-acre retreat, *Steigersruh* (Steiguer's Rest).[135] In 1824 he entertained

Philippe Suchard, Wikimedia Commons, public domain

Swiss visitors Philippe Suchard of Boudry, Canton Neuchâtel (whose American experiences inspired him to become a major Swiss chocolatier and who went on to form a Swiss colony of his own

---

[132] de Steiguer (1888), 14-15.

[133] Hoskins, 147.

[134] Gall, I, 168.

[135] de Steiguer, Rudolph, letter in French to L.-F. de R. in Bern during August 1821, published as "Colonie Suisse dans l' Amérique du Nord" in *Journal des Voyages, Découvertes et Navigations Modernes, un Archives Géographiques et Statistiques du XIX^{e}Siècle,* a periodical edited by *Société de Géographiques et de Voyageurs Français et Étrangers* (Paris: J.-T. Verneur, 1822), Vol. 13, 121-124.

called Alpina, near Harrisville, Lewis County, New York);[136] Dr. Joseph Bury (of Basil, Fairfield County, Ohio, named for Basel, Switzerland) also of Pittsburgh, Pennsylvania, and vicinity;[137] and Arnold Hauert/Howard of Wengi, Canton Bern, (born 1791 in Bern, son of piano-maker Joseph Hauert and Elisabeth Wyss, a relative of the Athens Wyss/Weiss family).[138] Howard had misgivings about America;[139] he later lived like a recluse in Monroe County, dying there in the infirmary in 1861. A fourth member of this party was Friedrich de Büren, whom Baron v. Steiger intended to marry to his daughter Elizabeth, but she fled right after the forced ceremony and eventually got it annulled. The Baron wrote glowing reports back to Switzerland, though later his grandson, Louis Philippe de Steiguer, characterized him as disillusioned and unfulfilled in the end, after many of his young unattached workers, unaccustomed to farm life, had deserted his wilderness colony and both his beloved Magdalena and his spiritual advisor Chaplain Thune died.

---

[136] Schelbert, Leo, and Rappolt, Hedwig, *Alles ist ganz anders hier: Auswandererschicksale in Briefen aus zwei Jahrhunderten* (Zurich: Limmat, 1984), Footnote 4: Section 2, 439.

[137] Schelbert and Rappolt, 187.

[138] Schelbert and Rappolt, 194-199.

[139] Schelbert, Leo, editor, *America Experienced: Eighteenth and Nineteenth Century Accounts of Swiss Immigrants to the United States*, (Camden, Maine: Picton Press, 1996), 191-192.

Ludwig Gall believed in doing virtuous deeds, but was seldom rewarded for his good intentions. He was a well-educated Catholic idealist who considered it his life's work to improve the lot of disadvantaged people. He wrote two thick volumes of travel descriptions about this 1819 emigration, his fruitless attempt to develop a colony in Pennsylvania in 1820, and his return to Trier in late 1820.

Gall had grandiose goals, but he was willing to put his altruistic ideals into practice. Because he had resigned his Prussian clerkship and citizenship, he was forbidden to recruit emigrants from his native Rhineland, which was now Prussian territory, so he turned to Switzerland, where there was extreme poverty and the authorities grudgingly permitted some emigration. During the emigration process for the Swiss, Gall served as a facilitator by corresponding with his emigration commission in Bern; arranging details on ship contracts in Antwerp; making sure the ships would be clean, safe, well-provisioned, and well-run; and following the progress of the emigration parties down the Rhine. He was energetic and eager, but naïve and gullible. He is regarded as a forerunner to Karl Marx (also from Trier) as an economic theorist, but did not consider himself a socialist and used a private stock company to fund his project. He carried his empathy for the working poor to the point of selling his own goods to benefit European emigrants, but earned ridicule as a chronic complainer.

Engraving of Edward Everett, Wikimedia Commons

As Edward Everett's review of Gall's book asserts, by Gall's own account "every man, woman, and child whom Gall approaches, defrauds him."[140] He considered himself a victim at every turn, but he probably looked like easy prey. Some of his grievances seem legitimate enough. In Europe he was dismayed by the insufficient numbers of travelers, the attitudes of his fellow commissioners, an attempt by Separatist elders to hoodwink him and his party, and the poor quality of the emigrants arriving at Antwerp; in America he was angry with price-gougers in the farmers' market, with dishonest shippers about charges, with swindlers at inns posing as innkeepers taking his money, with baggage handlers for moving his luggage without permission, with his fellow commissioners about their shares of the fares, and with his servants who robbed him. The year 1819 was a time of economic distress. But his negative attitudes hurt him in the end. The tone of his book was interpreted as "massive

---

[140] Everett, Edward, review of *My Emigration to the U. S. of N. America in the Spring of 1819, and my return home in the winter of 1820*, (Everett's translation of the title) by Ludwig Gall, 2 vols., 8vo., Treves, 1822, entitled "Schmidt and Gall in America," in *North American Review*, Vol. XVII, New Series, Vol. VIII, (Boston: O. Everett, 1823), 103 ff.

criticism of the United States"[141] and, being written in German and having adverse reviews, it was not widely read in America.

As one of the commissioners, Gall was aboard the ship, personally holding the captain to promised sanitation standards, requiring sufficient provisions under a set of rules suggested by his noble university friends von Gagern and von Fürstenwärther. Although Gall described his Swiss cohorts on the "*Eugénie*" as "smugglers, thieves, cheats, and prostitutes,"[142] some of them being ex-prisoners, not to mention experiencing an alarming episode with a dangerous Swiss knife-wielding passenger, there were no deaths on board. Because Captain Dirk Cornelisz de Groot's ship "April," with 400 passengers and a crew of 20 from Amsterdam on June 26, 1817, took on 640 more sick passengers from other vessels at Texel, including many Swiss from Canton Aargau,[143] hundreds of passengers were hospitalized with typhus and 70 more died on the passage to New Castle, Delaware, landing January 3, 1818, American officials dreaded the worst from other European ships.[144] The New York health inspectors were astonished to see when they came on board that everyone on the "*Eugénie*" was healthy and that there had been two births aboard. One child born in the Atlantic was fittingly named Jacob Eugen Ocean Fankhauser,[145] who could choose whether to be a citizen of France (born on a French ship), Switzerland (the native land of the parents), or the United States (the parents' next landing place); Christian Tüscher could only choose to be French or American because his whole family was expatriated from Switzerland.

---

[141] Barclay, David E., and Elisabeth Glaser-Schmidt, *Transatlantic Images and Perceptions: Germany and America Since 1776* (The German Historical Institute: Cambridge University Press, 1997), 69.

[142] Everett's translation in his review, 117.

[143] Swieringa, Robert, "Partial Passenger List of the Dutch Ship APRIL to New Castle, Delaware, June 1817," *The Palatine Immigrant* (Columbus, OH: March 1993, No. 18), 76-81.

[144] Cronau, Rudolph, *Denkschrift zum 150. Jahrestag der deutschen Gesellschaft der Stadt New York 1784-1934,* (New York: Chas. H. Bohn & Co., Inc., 1934), 64.

[145] Gall I, 244.

Jakob Tüscher and his son Abraham served as representatives for the 41 adults and 22 children aboard the "*Eugénie*" at the marine trial to justify why the unruly Swiss passenger, Franz Spittler, father-in-law of Niklaus Fankhauser, had to be shackled. Both Tüschers signed the findings together with the captain and officers. Spittler had threatened to throw Gall overboard (because Gall had the gall to expect him to work off his passage) and menaced Captain Jullou and everyone else on board with a knife and guns, forcing drastic measures during desperate moments, compelling the captain to make out a report for the French naval authorities.[146]

---

[146] Gall I, 318-323.

The Lasting Legacy: Plans versus Results

Tüscher and his party had decided in New Jersey to head for the Great Kanawha River and settle on Bruen's land in what was then Virginia (now West Virginia), but when they were stranded in Ohio they were persuaded to purchase government land near the Ohio River at Captina Creek (mangled as *Käptin*) and Buckhill Bottom (garbled as *Bogilboden*)[147] that had familiar terrain for Swiss people, including wooded hills up from the river bottoms, suitable for grazing. Despite the Swiss Great Council's conclusion that this emigration society was practically dissolved *("so gut wie aufgelöst")*,[148] there are many thousands of descendants of the original immigrants; Jacob Tisher himself left 117 descendants at his death[149] and the Fankhausers were even more prolific, leaving their robust gene pool in the settlement and beyond. The earliest Swiss surnames still exist in the area–Tisher, Fankhauser/Fankhouser, Tschappat, Marti(n), Nisperl(e)y, Ruegsegger/Resecker.

Frances Wright, an Englishwoman traveling in America at this time, perceives humble, rustic Swiss as better suited to American life than Englishmen corrupted by city life: "The starving emigrants of Switzerland and Germany are simple agriculturalists and ignorant peasants, who here quietly devote themselves to the pursuits from which they have been driven in Europe, and instantly become harmless and industrious citizens. Their prejudices, whatever they may be, are perfectly innocent, and of absolute vices they usually have none."[150] This little colony who became "harmless and industrious citizens" in the hinterlands of Ohio grew and attracted additional families, drawing substantial chain migration from

---

[147] Schelbert and Rappolt, note 12, 440.
[148] Cantonal Archive of Canton Bern, *Verwaltungsarchiv, Gemeinde- und Niederlassungswesen, Burger und Einwohner*, BB XIIIa 151, 30-31.
[149] Henke, [Rev.] H[enry], under heading *"Selig sind, die im Herrn sterben,"* report of death of Jacob Tüscher on 23 Apr 1860 in *Der Christliche Apologete*, Vol. XXII, No. 27, whole number 1120, (Cincinnati, July 5, 1860), 108.
[150] Wright, , Frances, *Views of Society and Manners in America; in a Series of Letters from that Country to a Friend in England During the Years 1818, 1819, and 1820, by an Englishwoman,* (London: Longman, Hurst, Reese, Orme, and Brown, 1821), 468.

Switzerland that added to its German Methodist, Reformed, and Apostolic Christian congregations. By 1860 there were already 846 Swiss-born in Monroe County and 91 in Belmont County, plus spillover into Marshall and Wetzel Counties, Virginia (now West Virginia), not counting thousands of American-born children and grandchildren.

Gall tried a noble experiment. In Europe he had advertised for shareholders in a prospective settlement between the 37th and 43rd parallels on the Mississippi, Missouri, or Ohio River, out of the flood plain and near mines or salt works, to be called *Rosenau* (Rose Meadow). Once in America, after he met a well-informed French officer in Brooklyn who explained the future trade implications of the Erie Canal, he decided to go no farther than Cincinnati and then select a site after scouting the possibilities. Using conventional European logic, he decided to assemble a new settlement society, something more than just a welfare society, in what seemed to be a sensible site for a headquarters, in a German-like climate, on the Susquehanna, a river even wider than Gall's familiar Rhine, in Harrisburg, Pennsylvania, the capital city of a major state, the state populated with more Germans than any other. Gall served as a secretary and member of the land committee. He recruited eighteen of the foremost German-speaking burghers for his society, with President Georg Lochmann, a Lutheran pastor; Vice-President Jacob Bucher, a state legislator; Treasurer Obed Fahnestock, Chief Burgess (equivalent to Mayor) of the borough of Harrisburg; and Gall's co-Secretary Friedrich Wilhelm Leopold, later Harrisburg's Clerk of Works. Some other influential members were Christian Gleim, later publisher of *The Pennsylvanian*; George Heisley/Heisely, a clock and instrument maker, a Burgess of Harrisburg, who chose the music to go with Francis Scott Key's poem "The Star-Spangled Banner" in 1814 by going through all the tunes in his flute songbook and choosing "To Anacreon in Heaven;" Melchior Rahm, state senator, innkeeper of the Franklin House and landlord of the Pennsylvania Inn; John Wiestling, publisher of *Die Härrisburger Morgenröthe*; and Georg Ziegler, a Harrisburg councilman.

But Gall was unable to cope with American frontier realities. Despite his best-laid plans, a natural location, and well-chosen associates, Gall's business plans failed in a terrible economy. And Gall, a wealthy foreigner, an "easy mark," was prosecuted for violating the Sunday "blue laws," a foreign concept to Europeans. He was sued successfully by his lazy indentured servant and his neighbors and merchants who trumped up charges against him and bought off witnesses with whiskey. He went home to Europe in the winter of 1820, disillusioned, and chronicled his experiences, limiting his encouragement of emigration to hard-working poor people, but strictly warning them of the perils. Always a promoter of the best chances for success, Gall advised venturesome emigrants to choose either northwest Pennsylvania with its natural resources or the rich basins of the Whitewater and Little Miami River basins in Ohio or Indiana.

Baron von Steiger first intended to form his settlement somewhere along the Red River and later chose present-day Indiana,[151] but his flatboat got stuck on a sandbar near Marietta, Ohio, altering his plans, so he purchased a substantial tract of Ohio Company land in Athens County. His beloved Magdalena's extended family–de Steiguer, Finsterwald,[152] Hausner, Junod,[153] Oberholzer, Stalder, Wyss–stayed in that county, but most of the unattached young craftsmen soon moved out of the untamed wilderness to more populous places where they could earn a living by practicing their trades.

Jean Labarthe's family eventually went to a culture that suited their French-speaking background, in Louisiana.

So our Swiss split into four groups and went their separate directions, each having to adapt to changes in plans, settling in familiar-looking landscapes, finding uncultivated frontiers to conquer, and working in their accustomed traditional methods. They left varying legacies: a lasting settlement of citizens in Monroe and Belmont Counties, Ohio, several families in Athens County, Ohio, an acculturated family in Louisiana, and an abortive attempt at a colony

---

[151] Lehmann, Mary Jean (Johnson), *The Family of Daniel Uhl II ...*, 129.
[152] "Finsterwald Family Early Athens Settlers," by C. H. Harris, *Athens Messenger*, (Athens, Ohio, January 4, 1952), 4.
[153] http://www.junod.ch/en/athens_eng.shtml, accessed July 24, 2016

in Arkansas. Unlike the Swiss, Ludwig Gall left his utopian dream behind when he gave up his rented Harrisburg mansion; he lived in Europe the rest of his life and had no children, but he leaves his own heritage of writings and inventions and ideas.

Passenger Lists

The following transcribed lists are for our two ships from Antwerp to New York in 1819. Conventional genealogy wisdom is that neither list should exist because New York passenger arrival lists were not kept until 1820 and Antwerp passenger departure lists do not exist for the 19th century except for the year 1855. Those are both true statements. By rights, neither should exist. The requirement to keep accurate maritime passenger lists beginning in 1820 was spurred by the sudden increase in the number of passengers and the tragic deaths due to disease and overcrowding, such as those on the "Aprill" in 1817 and 1818.

Astonishingly, good quality lists do exist for both ships, and the villages of origins of most of the passengers can be identified from them. The explanation is that Captain Jullou of the *"Eugénie"* returned the master's list to the ship's home port of Brest, France, per French navy regulations because he was still a naval officer, and the "Columbia" in 1819 continued from New York to its and Captain Kurtz's home port of Philadelphia, which had begun keeping baggage passenger lists in 1800.

The "*Eugénie*"

Etat Nominatif des Emigrantes Suisses et allemands au port d' Anvers l'embarquiants à bord de navire français L'Eugénie par les Etats-unis[154]

	Nomes des Domicile	Prénoms	de Age	Observations
01	Gall Treves*	Louis	28 ans	
02	Willwersch	Marie Son Epouse	18 id	id
03	Gall	Martin	52	id
04	Moers	Marg^te Son Epouse	51	id
05	Walder Sohlingen*	G^me ?ingt?	31	
06	Heckel	Fréd. G^me pharmé	18	[blank]
07	Liebeskind Weimar	Chrétien	20 commiss	

---

[154] *Les rôles d'équipage de l' « Eugénie »*, Service historique de la Défense, Brest, France, registre 2P7-169, rôle n°41.

08	Eberhard Marburg	Nicolas tanneur	19	
09	Kuhl	Henry boucher	19	id
10	Geit [Heit]	Thierry tanneur	19	id
11	Riehl	Philippe boucher	20	id
12	Mollenkopf Pfullingen	Jean chirurgus	29	
13	Houbar	Daniel tailleur	40	Liège
14	id	Adéle sa femme	39	id
15	id	Aug^te |ses enfants	13	id
16	id	Eugénie |ses enfants	04	id
17	VanDerVliet Anvers*	F^ois boulanger	29	
18	Pletscher Schaffhouse*	Martin Cultivateur	56	
19	id	Elisabeth Son Epouse	56	id
20	id	Féréna sa fille	30	id
21	Jung Rabach*	André menuisier	24	
22	Wiessel id	[Wissel]Pierre	20	id
23	Kopp Retzefile*	J^n George menuisier	35	
24	Gerock Unterreisersheim*	Jacques cultivateur	18	
25	Neuffer Horkheim	Chrêtien id	29	

26	Gravenstein Lonkgau*	Catherine id	22	
27	Neuffer Lockgau*	Christine	03	
28	Buck Obergriesbach?*	Jean Cult.	30	
29	Muller Schoray	JJ^ques * d.o	30	
30	Schaeffer d.o	Marg^te	30	id
31	Muller d.o	Chrét	03	id
32	Muller d.o	Frederick	01	id
33	Muller d.o	Catharine	20	id
34	Nonenmacher d.o	G^me	18	id
35	Zoll d.o	J^ques	43	Id
36	Reiterinn Heinsheim	Barbe d.o	35	
37	Zoll Schoray	Elise * d.o	15	
38	id d.o	J^ques	10	id
39	id d.o	Fréderick	½	id
40	Kubach Unterreisersheim*	JJ^ques d.o	43	
41	Heischlin? d.o	Régine	22	id
42	Frankhauser d.o	Danl	32	Trub
43	id d.o	Marie	25	id
44	id d.o	Danl	06	id

45	id		Jean	04	id
	d.o				
46	id		Madelaine	02	id
	d.o				
47	Spittler Twann*		Sophie d.o	21	
48	Frankhauser		Nicolas	38	Trub
	d.o				
49	Frankhauser		Nicolas	18	id
	d.o				
50	id		Louis	12	id
	d.o				
51	id		Susanne	11	id
	d.o				
52	id		J^n Werner	09	id
	d.o				
53	Frankhauser		J^n Arnold	07	Trub
	d.o				
54	id		Anne Marie	05	id
	d.o				
55	id		G^me	03	id
	d.o				
56	id		Cath^e	01	id
	d.o				
57	Tuscher Burenzumhof*		J^ques	43	
58	id	sa femme	Cath^e	29	id
59	id		Jean	10	id
60	id		J^ques	08	id
61	id		Anne	07	id
62	id		N^as	05	id
63	id		Marie	03	id
64	id		Abraham	22	id
65	id		Elise	25	id
66	id		J^ques	01	id

67	id	Elizab.	04	id
68	Marti Mulchie*	J^ques	71	
69	id	Jean	31	id
70	id	Chrétien	22	id
71	Huggi Zimisswald*	Benoit	38	
72	id sa femme	Marie	34	id
73	id	Samuel	10	id
74	id	Chrétien	09	id
75	id	Benoit	04	id
76	id	Rudolph	03	id
77	Dams? Anvers*	J^ques trottier?	27	
78	Stallaeis ?	[damaged]er	22 servante	id
79	Tschapp[damaged] Gotzingen*		34	cultivateur
80	id sa femme	[damaged]	35	id
81	id	[damaged]	13	id
82	id	Cath^e	11	id
83	Tschappat Gotzingen*	J^ques	~~34~~ 09	
84	id	M^ie Anne	06	id
85	id	Fréd^ck	02	id
86	Schneeder Burenzumhof*	Bénoit	43	
87	id sa femme	Barbe	39	id
88	id	J^ques	14	id
89	id	Elise	08	id
90	id	Benoit	05	id

91	id	Madel^ne	02	id
92	id	Jean	1 moi	id
93	Schmidt Brug*	Louis	24	~~Berne~~
94	Stamm Schaffhouse*	Martin	42	
95	id	Madelaine	39	id
96	id	Jean	09	id
97	id	Louis	04	id
98	id	Christine	02	id
99	id	Férena	11	id
100	id	Madelaine	07	id
101	Spittler	François	47	Twan*
102	Stamm	Madeleine	28	Berne
103	De Caen	L^uis Aug^te peintre	49	id
104	Mespelter Bruxelles*	Jeanne servante	29	
105	Cornett Anvers*	G^me Jos^h etudiant?	33	

Anvers, le 22. Mai 1819
pour Copie Conforme F Jullou

The French captain, Jullou, translated common German forenames and place names of large localities into their standard French equivalents with no trouble, such as Ludwig to Louis, Barbara to Barbe, Bendicht to Bénoit, Magdalena to Madelaine, and Schaffhausen to Schaffhouse. Understandably, he had considerable trouble interpreting the old German handwriting style from passengers' travel documents. As examples, he erroneously transcribed B as G in Bözingen, h as k in Löchgau, z as r in Schozach, and ch as y in Schozach, and misspellings are common in his list. Somewhat fittingly, his name gets misspelled in various documents and newspapers as Frillon, Jallan, Jallou, Jullan, Jullon, Jullow, etc.

E01	Treves (French) is German or English Trier
E05	Johlingen might be Jöhlingen, Baden; this could also be Sohlingen or Solingen
E17, 77, 105	Anvers (French) is English Antwerp
E18	Schaffhouse (French) is German or English Schaffhausen, Canton Schaffhausen, Switzerland
E21	Rabach is [Mömbris-]Rappach, Unterfranken, Bavaria
D23	Retzefile, spelled Retzefeld by Gall, probably Ritzenfeld near Sulzbach/Oberpfalz, Bavaria
E24	Unterreisersheim is Untereisesheim, Württemberg
E26, E27	Lonkgau and Lockgau both refer to Löchgau, Württemberg
E29	Obergriesbach is uncertain, maybe Obergruppenbach, Württemberg
E29, 37	Schoray is [Ilsfeld-]Schozach, Württemberg
E47, 101	Twan is Twann, Canton Bern (German) = Douanne, Canton Berne (French)
E57, 86	Burenzumhof is Büren zum Hof, Canton Bern
E68	Mulchie is Mülchi, formerly known as Mühlheim, Canton Bern
E71	Zimisswald is Zimmerwald, Canton Bern
E79, 83	Gotzingen is Bözingen, Canton Bern = Boujean, Canton Berne (French)
E93	Brug is unidentified, possibly Brügg, Canton Bern, or Brugg, Canton Aargau, or Bruges/Brugge, Belgium
E104	Bruxelles (French) is Brussels (English)

Except for a stroke of extremely good luck, this list would not exist. Ludwig Gall lost a pouch with all the essential travel documents for the Swiss. Along a road between Allondrelle la Malmaison, France, and Attert, Belgium, the horse tripped and threw off Gall's post rider, thrusting his chest into a rock and knocking him unconscious. The frightened horse bolted and ran away. Suddenly faced with an ethical dilemma, Gall chose to be the Good Samaritan and help one wounded postilion immediately by the side of the road rather than try to catch up with the horse and the saddlebag carrying all the official papers vital to a hundred others. After Gall revived the postilion and took him to an inn in town, where he recovered sufficiently, they both went looking for the postilion's horse. The two of them had been riding and searching for an hour as twilight finally turned to darkness when suddenly in the distance the post horse heard its rider's familiar voice talking to Gall (ironically, forebodingly telling Gall about a disaster: the roadside memorial for a man who was murdered by robbers at that point on the road), and it whinnied in response and came running.[155]

It was a make-or-break moment. Without the neighing of the horse in the dark in the distance, to Gall's (and our) profound relief, the travel papers would have been lost, and without papers nobody could have been transported. They would not have become trans-Atlantic passengers, but would have suffered an unknown fate in Europe. There would be no captain's list for them. All their current descendants would not exist. Their history would not exist. This book would not exist.

---

[155] Gall I, 137-138.

The "Columbia"

Report and manifest of the Cargo on board Ship Columbia of Philadelphia whereof Daniel L Kurtz Master burthen 2637/95(?) Tons built at Port Elizabeth State of New Jersey / owned by Henry Delar(?) of Philadelphia which cargo was taken on board at Antwerp and bound to New York as per Register No. 27 saved at Philadelphia on 27 March 1817.

Names of Passengers on board the Ship Columbia Daniel L Kurtz master from Antwerp to Newyork

01 ~~Benjamin Hicks~~ at Newyork	26	Liverpool	Trader
02 Rudolph Steiger Gentleman	40	Berne	
03 Magdalena	30	"	
04 Rudolph	14	"	
05 Wilhelmina	16	"	
06 Elisabeth	10	"	
07 ~~Samuel Reichenbach~~ at Newyork	46	id. "	Notary
08 Albert August "	13	"	

09 John Labarthe	55	Geneva	Trader
10 Joanna Leonore	50	"	
11 Susan Margaret	23	"	
12 John Joseph	16	"	
13 Francis Philip	15	"	
14 August	13	"	
15 ~~Peter Thomas Oudra~~ ? at Newyork	24	"	Trader
16 ~~Andrew Delpeche~~ ? do.	21	"	do.
17 Jacob Schtalder	62	Luzelfluh	farmer
18 Anna	40	"	
19 Frederick	15	"	
20 Peter	13	"	
21 Georges	12	"	
22 Nicolas	09	"	
23 Andrew	[blot]	"	
24 Elisabeth	[blot]	"	
25 Catharine	19	"	
26 Rosina	18	"	
27 Jacob Finsterwald	30	Berne	farmer
28 Alois Oberholzer	32	"	Miller
29 Ursala	25	"	
30 Henry	05	"	
31 David Hausner	50	Berne	farmer
32 Barbara	35	"	
33 Elisabeth	16	"	
34 Maria	13	"	
35 Anna	09	"	
36 Adam Eberhard	37	Gravenried	Taylor
37 Anna "	35	"	
38 ~~Louise Äberhardt~~ ? Newyork	33	"	Servant
39 Oswald Martin	23	Berne	Taylor

40 Anna "	35	"	
41 John Jenser	53	"	Butcher
42 Christian Mossimann Weaver	46	Soumiswald	
43 Jacob Kocher	23	~~Berne~~ Bure	Potter
44 Jacob Sutter	23	"	Taylor
45 Rudolph Gribi	22	"	Sadler
46 Jacob Weiss?	19	Berne	do.
47 Rudolph Webel	30	Bure	Farmer
48 Anna "	23	Bure	"
49 John "	08	"	
50 Rudolph "	05	"	
51 Maria "	06	"	
52 Mathias Kuster	51	"	Shoemaker
53 Nicolas "	21	"	"
54 ~~Louis Gribi~~ Newyork	53	"	vintner
55 ~~Mathias? Keiser~~ do	19	Schafhouse	Tanner
56 ~~Francis~~ L—	[blot] 1	Berne	Taylor d.o
57 ~~Maria~~ "	[blot] 9	"	d.o
58 Bernard Walter	58	Muhlendorf	farmer
59 Charles Prince	_	Neufchatel	Sadler

Captain Kurtz lists the occupations in English, but he uses the French versions of place names for communities that are mostly German, though he himself was German-born. Liverpool is English, of course, and Geneva and Neuchatel are in French-speaking areas of Switzerland, but the other places are in German-speaking Switzerland. The captain seems to have taken his list from travel documents in French. His Soumiswald is Sumiswald in German, Schafhouse is Schaffhausen, Luzelfluh is Lützelflüh, Gravenried is Grafenried, Bure is Büren an der Aare, where the surnames Kocher, and Sutter, and Gribi, from "Bure," all have citizenship rights.

Passport List of District of Fraubrunnen, Canton Bern, 1819

E57-E63
No. 350
Surname Tüscher
Forename Jakob, with wife & children & nanny
Citizen previously Büren z. Hoof
Church ---
Occupation ex-agent
Destination The United States of North America
Date April 7
Expiration to make future citizenship in the above country
Trip's Purpose via Antwerp or Amsterdam

E68-E70
No. 351
Surname Marti
Forename Jakob, and his two sons Johann and Christen Marti
Citizen Mülchi/Messen
Church Messen
Occupation butcher
Destination ditto The United States of North America
Date April 10
Expiration ditto to make future citizenship in the above country
Trip's Purpose ditto via Antwerp or Amsterdam

E64-E67
No. 352
Surname Tüscher
Forename Abraham, with his wife and 2 children
Citizen previously Büren z. Hoof
Church ---
Occupation ex-agent
Destination ditto The United States of North America
Date ditto April 10
Expiration ditto to make future citizenship in the above country
Trip's Purpose ditto via Antwerp or Amsterdam

E86
No. 353
Surname Schneider
Forename Bendicht (note: E87-E92 wife and children not on list)
Citizen ditto Büren z. Hoof
Church ditto Büren z. Hoof
Occupation farm worker
Destination ditto The United States of North America
Date ditto April 10
Expiration ditto to make future citizenship in the above country

Trip's Purpose   ditto via Antwerp or Amsterdam

C36-C37
No. 354
Surname Aeberhard
Forename J[ohanne]s Adam and his wife
Citizen Graff[enrie]d
Church Graff[enrie]d
Occupation farm worker
Destination ditto The United States of North America
Date ditto April 10
Expiration ditto to make future citizenship in the above country
Trip's Purpose ditto via Antwerp or Amsterdam

The Individuals in their Communities

Emigrants who chose to come to America were those who were unable or unwilling to cope with conditions in their home environment. Those brought to the decision were the unwanted, the rebels, the desperate, the adventurers, and the free spirits, and many of these risk-takers soon became developers and builders of their new environs.

It is no rarity to find children born out of wedlock or shortly after marriage. The Swiss church courts, associated with the government, adamantly guarded their conventional morals and severely punished violations.

Pregnancy or birth during emigration was seemingly no barrier to travel. Life went on during the arduous journey. Six children were born among Tüscher's Monroe/Belmont group during 1819: Johannes Schneider in March or April en route to Antwerp, Maria Hugi on May 11, Jacob Eugen Ocean Fankhauser (Daniel's) on May 29 aboard ship, Anna Margaretha Rügsegger on June 26 in Le Havre, Christian Tüscher (Jakob's) in June or July aboard ship, and Elisabetha Fankhauser (Niklaus's) on October 9 after arriving in Ohio.

As you look at these family groups, keep in mind the Swiss legal system. As the most obvious example, in Bern, the penalty for being an apostate (Anabaptist, Mennonite, Amish, *Wiedertäufer*, *Taufgesinnte*) was exile in 1695, and imprisonment, galley slavery, whippings, or death after 1709. Most either converted or acquiesced; the few Anabaptists who remained lived mainly in rough mountainous areas considered marginal for settlement even by Swiss standards. The Steiger group followed his lead in the Reformed faith; the Tüscher group had varying degrees of conformity to the church/state rules; some Fankhausers were constables and prison guards, and some Tüschers and Spittlers were prisoners. Both leaders, though, had violated the Bernese marriage and divorce rules.

The first Swiss families in Monroe and Belmont Counties included:

Passenger List of the "*Eugénie*" Antwerp to New York 1819, French military archives, Brest

[In the following, E indicates the "*Eugénie*," C the "Columbia," and the number is the line in the list. Digitized church books are available online for Canton Bern at http://www.query.sta.be.ch/archivplansuche.aspx, Staatliche Sammlung, Kirchenbücher. They are also available online at Family History Centers and members of partner organizations, as well as on FHL microfilm. Records are systematic, chronological, and indexed.]

E57 Jakob **Tüscher/Jacob Tisher**, born out of wedlock on 25 Mar 1777 in Schalunen, Canton Bern, to the weaver Niklaus Tüscher (described as "*blöd im Verstand*," simple-minded, so did not sign at the mandatory oath-taking in 1798) of Büren zum Hof, Canton Bern, and Anna Sterchi of Schalunen; Jakob was legitimized on 20 Nov 1790. He was married 1st on 16 Aug 1796 in Payerne, Canton Vaud, to Jeanne Marie Brossy. They were divorced on 31 Aug 1812; Jeanne Marie then married 2nd August Vuille of LaSagne, Canton Neuchâtel, in Limpach, Canton Bern, on 18 May 1814; she died on 24 Jan 1816 in Büren zum Hof, Canton Bern, and August Vuille died 28 Jan 1816 in Büren zum Hof.

Jakob Tüscher's only child with Jeanne Marie was Abra(ha)m born 1797; see below.

While still legally married to Jeanne Marie, Jakob fathered a child with Elisabeth **Arn** (born 12 Dec 1784 in Wangenried, Canton Bern, baptized 19 Dec 1784 Wangen an der Aare, Canton Bern), named Maria, born 23 Oct 1809 in Wangenried and baptized 31 Oct 1809 at Wangen, who died on 12 Dec in Wangenried and was buried on 14 Dec 1809 at Wangen.

Jakob Tüscher also had children with his wife or housekeeper, as described below:

E58 Katharina **Winterberger**, born 17 Feb 1790 at "Stein" in Meiringen, Canton Bern, baptized 21 Feb 1790 at Meiringen, Canton Bern.

A manuscript family group sheet from Ernst Winterberger indicates that Katharina Winterberger of Meiringen was "married to Jacob Tüscher," but with no dates.[156] The March 1819 passport register from Fraubrunnen (for foreign consumption) hedges a bit, listing *"Jakob Tüscher, seine Frau & Kinder und 1 Kindermagd,"* "his wife & children and a nanny."[157] The passenger list of Captain Jullou in Antwerp describes Catherine Tuscher as *"sa femme"* (his wife). They may have had a civil ceremony in Antwerp, when they were no longer prohibited from marrying by the Swiss law.

E59 Johannes, born 20 Jan 1810 at Mülchi, Canton Bern, *married Philippina Maienknecht.*

E60 Jakob, born 10 Jun 1811 at Mülchi, Canton Bern, *married Catharina Bauer.*

---

[156] Family History Library Special Collection, heir Ernest Winterberger, MS 795.

[157] Staatsarchiv Kanton Bern, Bern, Switzerland, Verwaltungsarchiv, *Kontrolle der vom Oberamt Fraubrunnen ausgestellten grösseren Reisepässe*, B XIII 503, unpaginated, entry number 350 for Jakob Tüscher, 7 Apr 1819.

E61 Anna, born 24 Sep 1812 at Reiben, under French rule, *married Johann Durs Suter.*

E62 Nicklaus, born 26 Apr 1814 at Reiben, under French rule, *married Rosina Dubach/Rosanna Tubaugh.*

E63 Maria, born 17 May 1816 in the *Frauenarbeitshaus* (women's workhouse) in Bern, baptized 30 May 1816 in the *Heiliggeistkirche* (Holy Ghost Church) in Bern, *married Jacob Maienknecht, who was in the Harmonie Society from September 1830 to 1832.*[158]

Christian was born ca Jun or Jul 1819 on the Atlantic aboard the ship *"Eugénie."* He married Mary Ellen Rhodes.

E64 Abraham **Tüscher**, of Büren zum Hof, Canton Bern, was baptized on 12 Oct 1797 at Payerne, Canton Vaud, named with an Old Testament name after his maternal grandfather Abram Brossy; Abraham was married on 10? or 20? Sep 1814, resident at Reiben, under French rule, by Pastor Richard at Payerne to

E65 Elisabeth **Marti,** of Mülchi in the church parish of Messen, Canton Bern (later Canton Solothurn), baptized 1 Jan 1791, daughter of E68, Jacob Marti.

E67 Daughter Elisabeth, born 25 May 1815 at Mülchi, baptized 4 Jun 1815 at Messen, *married Martin Voegtly.*

E66 Son Jakob, born 3 Oct 1818 at Payerne, baptized 18 Oct 1818 at Limpach.

Maria Anna *married Samuel Noll.*

E48 Niklaus **Fankhauser** of Trub, Canton Bern, baptized 12 May 1782, emigrated with 8 small children and the great ocean before him (*acht kleine Kinder hatte ich vor mir und den großen Ozean,*)[159] and by 1852 had 21 children and 43 grandchildren. He hoped to find a place for his family to live without being turned away by landlords because he had so many children.

---

[158] Pitzer, Donald E., and Leigh Ann Chamness, eds., *Georg Rapp's Disciples, Pioneers and Heirs: A Register of the Harmonists in America*, (Evansville, IN: The University of Southern Indiana Press, 1994), 148 (entry number 917).

[159] "Schreiben eines Berner Landmanns aus dem Staate Ohio in Nordamerika" dated 29 Mar 1852, in *Christlicher Volksbote aus Basel,* (Basel, Switzerland: Basler Missionsgesellschaft, 23 Jun 1852) No. 25, 195.

He first had an out-of-wedlock son, his namesake, with Barbara **Läd(e)rach**, who was baptized 7 May 1783 at Worb, Canton Bern,

E49 Niklaus, born 14 Aug 1801 at Worb, Canton Bern, declared illegitimate 25 Sep 1801, emigrated with his father and stepmother, *married Anna Roth.*

Niklaus Sr. was married 1st on 8 Jan 1806 in Bern, Canton Bern, to Anna **Pfister** of Trachselwald, Canton Bern, baptized 21 Oct 1788 at Kirchdorf, Canton Bern.

E50 Carl Ludwig, baptized 23 May 1806 in Bern.

E51 Susanna Maria, baptized 8 Sep 1807 in Bern.

E52 Johann Werner, born 8 Feb 1810, baptized 18 Feb, 1810 in Bern, *married Barbara Koertz.*

E53 Johann Samuel Arnold "Andy," born 30 Jan 1812 in Bern, baptized 9 Feb 1812 in Bern.

E54 Anna Maria, born 5 Apr 1814, baptized 10 Apr 1814 in Muri, Canton Bern.

E55 Rudolf Wilhelm, born 4 May 1816, baptized 12 May 1816 in Bern, *married Priscilla Smith and Rachel Kirkpatrick.*

E56 Maria Catharina, born 7 Jan 1818, baptized 9 Jan 1818 in Bern, *married Henry Minamyer.*

Niklaus Sr. was married 2nd ca 1818/1819 to

E47 Sophia **Spittler** (according to family lore she was in prison where Niklaus was a guard), who was baptized 27 May 1798, at Twann/Douanne, Canton Bern, pregnant during the journey with Elisabetha, a child born 9 Oct 1819 in Ohio.[160]

E101 Sophia's father Franz **Spittler**, baptized 23 Mar 1772 at Twann/Douanne, Canton Bern, was married 4 Jul 1794 at Twann, to *Maria Elisabeth Mürset(h) of Twann, who was baptized 8 Jul 1762 at Twann and died 4 Jan 1812 at Twann.*

E42 Daniel **Fankhauser** of Trub, Canton Bern, baptized 5 May 1776, brother of Niklaus, proclamations of banns on 5, 12, and 19 Jul 1812, married on 1 Aug 1812 at Bern in the Nydegg church.

---

[160] The Fankhauser section is based largely on the documentation in Miriam K. (Berlekamp) Fankhauser, *The Fankhausers of Monroe County, Ohio,* (Green Springs, OH: Echo Press, 1983), also FamilySearch microfilms/Bern digitizations.

E43 Maria **Wahli**, born at Ittigen, Canton Bern, baptized 2 Feb 1794 at Bolligen, Canton Bern.
E44 Daniel born 16 Dec, baptized 17 Dec 1812 in Muri.
E45 Johannes born 13 Aug, baptized 20 Aug 1815 in Muri.
E46 Magdalena born 24 Sep 1817, baptized 5 Oct 1817 in Muri.
Jacob Eugen Ocean was born 29 May 1819 at 2 a.m. on the Atlantic Ocean near the southwestern English coast at 49 degrees 39 minutes north latitude and 4 degrees 28 minutes west longitude, *married Anna Louise Burgenthal, died 13 Dec 1889 in Keokuk, Iowa.*
Daniel Sr. died 30 Mar 1850 after having consumption for 11 months. 14 children and 18 grandchildren were living as of 1852.

E68 Jacob **Marti(n)**, baptized 3 Mar 1747 at Mülchi = Mühlheim, Canton Bern,
married on 15 April 1783 to Rosina **Gerber** of Steffisburg, Canton Bern, who was baptized on 10 Apr 1767 "in den Erlen" at Steffisburg, at the time of her marriage a resident of Canton Neuchatel.
Jacob, born in Mülchi, baptized 9 Jul 1786 at Messen, Canton Bern, emigrated later, see below.
E69 Johannes, born in Mülchi, baptized 17 Aug 1788 at Messen.
(E65) Elisabeth, born in Mülchi, baptized 1 Jan 1791 at Messen, wife of Abraham Tüscher, see above.
E70 Christen, born in Mülchi, baptized 13 Feb 1795 at Messen. Christen was reportedly the first passenger to sight land from the middle mast of the "*Eugénie*" on 20 Jul 1819.

Members of this family who followed later in a "chain migration" were:

Jacob **Marti(n)** (Jr.) of Mühlheim = Mülchi, Canton Bern, baptized on 9 Jul 1786 at Messen, Canton Bern (now Canton Solothurn), married 14 Jun 1812
Maria **Feller**, born in Noflen, Canton Bern, baptized 25 Mar 1791 at Kirchdorf, Canton Bern.
 Elisabeth, born 13 Feb 1814 in Kirchthurnen, Canton Bern, baptized 20 Feb 1814 at Thurnen, Canton Bern.

Jacob, born 11 Mar, baptized 17 Mar 1815 at Kirchberg, Canton Bern, *married Anna Margaretha Rüegsegger.*

Johannes, born 4 Nov, baptized 17 Nov 1816 at Grafenried, Canton Bern.

E71 Bendicht **Hugi**, born at Obermühlern, Canton Bern, baptized 11 Jan 1781 at Zimmerwald, Canton Bern. After banns on 23 and 30 Jul and 6 Aug 1809 he was married on 11 Aug 1809 at Zimmerwald to

E72 Maria **Sebel**, born ca 1784 presumably at Bussy-Chardonney, Canton Vaud (the only Swiss locality where the surname Sebel has citizenship rights).

E73 Samuel, born 14 Mar 1811, baptized 24 Mar 1811 at Zimmerwald.

E74 Christen, baptized 15 Nov 1812 at Zimmerwald.

E75 Bendicht, born 30 Apr 1814, baptized 15 May 1814 at Zimmerwald.

E76 Rudolf, born 4 Jan, baptized 14 Jan 1816 at Zimmerwald.

Maria, born 11 May 1819 probably in Antwerp, after Captain Jullou's passenger list had been made out.

E79 Jacob **Tschäppätt**, nicknamed "Bonaparte," born 11 Dec 1784 in Bözingen/Boujean, Canton Bern, near Biel/Bienne, Canton Bern, laborer on the Mett estate. He was married 28 Nov 1804 at Bözingen to

E80 Barbara **Baumgartner**, citizen of Trub, Canton Bern, who was born 8 Oct 1782 in Bözingen.

E81 Jacob, born 27 Jan 1805 in Bözingen, baptized 3 Feb 1805 at Biel.

E82 Catharina, born 1 Jan 1807 in Bözingen, baptized 11 Jan 1807 at Biel.

E83 Johannes Emanuel, born 27 Sep 1810 in Bözingen, baptized 7 Oct 1810 at Biel.

E84 Marianne, born 4 May 1813 in Bözingen, baptized 16 May 1813 at Biel, Canton Bern.

Susanna, born ca 1815 in Biel or Bözingen, presumably died in Europe

E85 Friedrich, born ca 1817 presumably in Biel or Bözingen.

E86 Bendicht **Schneider** of Büren zum Hof, Canton Bern, baptized 18 Oct 1777 in Limpach, Canton Bern. He was married on 14 Mar 1800 in Limpach to

E87 Anna Barbara **Spaar**, baptized 25 Mar 1780 in Herzogenbuchsee, Canton Bern.

Joseph, baptized 21 Mar 1802, died 18 Mar 1811 in Limpach.

E88 Jakob, baptized 7 Oct 1804 in Limpach.

Johannes, born 29 Jun 1808, baptized 10 Jul 1808, died 19 Jan 1815 in Limpach.

E89 Elisabeth, born 15 Jul, baptized 21 Jul 1811 in Limpach.

E90 Bendicht, born 13 Jul, baptized 24 Jul 1814 in Büren zum Hof.

E91 Magdalena, born 5 Feb, baptized 16 Feb 1817 in Büren zum Hof.

E92 Johannes, born ca March/April 1819 en route to Antwerp.

Originally with Tüscher, but came on the *"Columbia"* with v. Steiger: Adam **Äberhardt/Eberhard** of Grafenried, Canton Bern, baptized 4 Jan 1784, Grafenried, Canton Bern. He was married on 27 Feb 1806 at Kirchberg, Canton Bern, to Anna Barbara **Glanzmann**, baptized 28 May 1767 at Hasle bei Burgdorf, divorced from Jacob **Aeschbacher** of Rüderswyl/Rüderswil, Canton Bern. She was the daughter of an Anna Glanzmann of Hasle bei Burgdorf, Canton Bern.

A Mr. **Eberhard**, E08 on the *"Eugénie,"* mentioned in Captain Jullot's protocol of the Spittler trial, is Nicolas Eberhard of Marburg, Hessen, of a different family from the Niklaus Eberhardt of Büren zum Hof, Canton Bern, who was killed by the French in 1798, and this Adam Eberhard from Grafenried, Canton Bern.

Others among the early core Swiss pioneers in Monroe/Belmont Counties in Ohio were:

Johann Jacob Benedikt **Nüsperli** (Nisperly, Nusperly), born 19 Jun 1800 and baptized 29 Jun 1800, of Aarau, Canton Aargau, unmarried, a fourth cousin to Anna Elisabeth "Nanny" Nüsperli, the wife of the "father of modern Switzerland," Swiss patriot (though Magdeburg-born) Heinrich Zschokke, the editor of the influential *Schweizer-Bote* newspaper in Aarau. Jacob Nüsperli went back to Switzerland in the spring of 1823 and brought his parents and siblings to America, namely:

Bendicht **Nüsperli**, his father, born 19 Jun 1763 in Aarau, Canton Aargau, a second lieutenant, butcher and swordsmith, *married 1st on 21 Mar 1790 to Maria Magdalena Rüffli, who married 2nd Johann Jacob Schmid after they were divorced.*

Maria Magdalena Nüsperli, young Jacob's half-sister, born 28 Apr 1795 in Aarau to his father's 1st wife, her namesake,

Bendicht was married 2nd on 8 Oct 1801 (already having fathered two children with her) in Locarno, Canton Tessin, to

Rosina **Hässig**, born 11 Dec 1768 in Aarau, baptized 13 Dec 1768 in Aarau.

Samuel Nüsperli, his brother, born 14 Aug 1798 in Aarau, baptized 17 Aug 1798 in Aarau, and Samuel's wife

Margaretha **Hässig**, born 3 May 1801 in Aarau.

Maria Rosina Nüsperli, born 31 Oct 1802 in Aarau, died 24 Jan 1803.

Ludwig Nüsperli, his brother, born 4 Dec 1803 in Aarau, *married Francisca Lucas.*

Johann Georg Nüsperli, born 9 Jun 1805 in Aarau, died 20 Mar 1808 in Aarau[161].

Christen **Rügsegger,** baptized 9 Jul 1779, of a dairying family (since 1733) at the *"Feldmatt"* near Röthenbach im Emmental, Canton Bern, who came via Le Havre, France, to Monroe County in 1819,

married on 9 May 1797 to Barbara **Moser** born 9 Aug/Sep? 1780 "im Hilchli" at Rüschegg, Canton Bern, baptized 13 Aug/Sep? 1780 at Steffisburg, Canton Bern, died 1854.

Johannes Rügsegger b. 1799 (the eldest, stayed in Switzerland).

Elisabeth Rügsegger b. 1800, *stayed in Switzerland, married 1st Christian Scharin, 2nd Peter Salzmann.*

Samuel Rügsegger born 1802, died 1806.

Christen/Christian Rügsegger, born 25 Apr 1804 "auf Ryffersegg" near Röthenbach im Emmental, Canton Bern, baptized 6 May 1804 at Röthenbach.

---

[161] The Nüsperli section is based on http://www.bernergeschlechter.ch/humogen/list.php?database=humo_&pers_lastname=N%C3%BCsperli&pers_prefix=EMPTY&part_lastname=equals

Barbara Rügsegger, born 26 Dec 1805 "auf Ryffersegg," baptized 12 Jan 1806 at Röthenbach, married E70 Christen Marti.

Susanna Rügsegger born 1808, stayed in Switzerland, *married Johannes Spycher.*

Peter Rügsegger, baptized 18 Aug 1809 at Röthenbach, *married Laura Hannah Powell.*

Samuel Rügsegger, born 10 Jul 1812 "auf Ryffersegg," baptized 24 Jul 1812 at Röthenbach.

Ulrich Rügsegger, born 1814, died 1814.

Friederich Rügsegger, born 16 Jan 1816 "auf Ryffersegg," baptized 26 Jan 1816 at Röthenbach.

Anna Margaretha Rügsegger, born 26 Jun 1819 in Le Havre, France, *married Jacob Marti.*

Note: On 15 Feb 1836 Mstr. Christian Rügsegger of Monro Caunte Staat Ohio Postoffis Fisching Krik [sic] writes to his brother Mstr. Niclaus Rugsegger by Bethlehem Stark Caunte Ohio [sic], mentioning the death of their parents, and that lately Niclaus has come to America.[162]

Later two brothers of Niklaus and Daniel Fankhauser also came to Ohio and raised large families, namely:

Johannes **Fankhauser**, of Trub, Canton Bern, born in the Brunnadern section of the city of Bern, baptized 5 May 1776 at Muri, Canton Bern, confirmed 30 March 1793 in the Nydegg Church in Bern, emigrated in 1824; died 1 May 1847, leaving 14 children and 15 grandchildren.

married in Bern (Nydegg church) on 8 May 1813 to Catharina **Simon** of Zollikofen, Canton Bern, who had been confirmed on 2 Apr 1809, Easter Sunday, at Bremgarten, Canton Aargau.

Catharina, born 16 Feb 1819, baptized 28 Feb 1819 at Muri, Canton Bern, was named for Catharina Winterberger, Jakob Tüscher's wife,

---

[162] Letter obtained from the late postal historian Jerry B. Devol, Marietta, OH, photocopies in possession of author and family of Howard G. Phillips and Shirley Brague Phillips, late of Hilliard, OH, who toured Switzerland with the author in 1986.

who was the child's baptismal sponsor just six weeks before Catharina Winterberger Tüscher left for America.

Samuel **Fankhauser**, of Trub, Canton Bern, baptized 27 Jun 1784, died August 1851, who went to Winesburg, Holmes County, OH, in 1835, married 18 Sep 1819 Anna Barbara Balz divorced Zaugg of Langnau, Canton Bern.
Anna, baptized 14 Jul 1819.
Maria, baptized 20 Aug 1820.
Samuel, baptized 2 Mar 1823.
Niklaus, born 21 Aug 1825, baptized 11 Sep 1825 in Bern.
Christian, born 15 Oct 1827, baptized 4 Nov 1827 in Köniz.
Elisabetha, born 20 Jan 1830, baptized 31 Jan 1830 in Köniz.
Maria Elisabeth, born and baptized 21 Aug 1831 in Köniz.
Friedrich, born and baptized 23 Nov 1834 in Köniz.

The principal Swiss settlers in the wilderness of Athens County were the following:

(Baron) Johann Rudolph **v. Steiger/de Steiguer de Granson**, of Switzerland, son and namesake of a member of the Grosser Rath (Great Council) of Bern, born on 29 Sep 1778 in Bern, Captain of the Guard in Karlsruhe for Karl Friedrich, the Grand-Duke of Baden, who had visited a v. Steiger family in Switzerland during a trip in 1775. He died on 22 Oct 1834 in Wood County, (now West) Virginia.

The Baron did something unheard of by marrying somebody from the working class (twice), 1st in 1803 Maria Louise Wilhelmine **Müller**, born on 8 Jul 1783 in Karlsruhe, Baden, daughter of a grand-ducal court gardener, then divorced her because of her adultery; *she in turn married 2nd) 14 Jan 1813 Samuel **Stettler** in Bern; that couple had Louise Stettler born 1810 out of wedlock, Karl Sigmund born 1813, Edmund born 1815, Maria Wilhelmine born 1816, and Eugen Rudolf born 1822; she died in 1827 in Bern.*
Johann Rudolph **de Steiguer** and Maria Louise Wilhelmine Müller had three children, who all were brought to America with their father:

1. Daughter Wilhelmine, born 11 Jan 1803 baptized on 14 Jan 1803 in Karlsruhe, Baden, married 1) 20 May 1823 Wood County, Virginia, David **Uhl** (who had served as a translator for the Baron in a court case, a tough German-speaking descendant of the 1754 immigrant Georg David **Uhl** baptized 3 Apr 1731 in Bretten, Baden)[163]; died 1853 in Harmar (now part of Marietta), Washington County, Ohio; married 2) 12 Apr 1850 Washington County, Ohio, William **Fahnestock** (called Fanshe on the marriage records), rumored to have strangled her for her inherited property, based on finger marks allegedly visible on her neck at the time of her death.
2. Son Johann Rudolph, baptized 30 May 1805 at Bern, Switzerland, died 19 Nov 1864 St. Louis, Missouri, on a business trip.
3. Daughter Elisabetha Magdalena, born 17 Apr 1808 and baptized 7 May 1808 Bern, Switzerland, died 1836 Athens County, married 1st at age 16 against her wishes in a marriage arranged by her father to Frederick de Buren of Lausanne, Switzerland, on 21 Sep 1824, but she escaped on her wedding day, never lived nor cohabited with him, and obtained a legislative annulment on 28 Jan 1829 introduced from the Judiciary Committee by Arius Nye,[164] of Campus Martius, the first abode of Ohio's 48 pioneers;[165] she later married Judge Leonidas Jewett on 26 Dec 1832.

Johann Rudolph von Steiger reportedly married 2nd Magdalena Stalder in May 1819 in Antwerp.[166]

Jacob **Stalder**, called "Papa" by the Baron, of Lützelflüh, Canton Bern, born on *Hof Lehn*, near Rüegsbach, part of the *Grüterhof,* in the Trachselwald region, Canton Bern, property of the Stalder family

---

[163] Lehmann, 118.

[164] *Acts of A General Nature, Passed at the First Session of the Twenty-seventh General Assembly of the State of Ohio: Begun and Held in the Town of Columbus December 1, 1828,* (Columbus, OH: Olmsted, Ballache and Camron, State Printers, 1829), 259.

[165] Bowman, Mary L., *Abstracts and Extracts of the Legislative Acts and Resolutions of the State of Ohio, Volumes 20 to 29: 1821-1831,* (Mansfield, OH: The Ohio Genealogical Society, 1996), 239-240.

[166] Gall I, 357.

since Elisabeth Muster married a Stalder in 1540,[167] baptized 13 Feb 1756 at Affoltern, Canton Bern; died in 1826 in Athens County, was married 1st ca 1776 at Rüegsau, Canton Bern, to
Anna **Hügli** of Sumiswald, Canton Bern, who was baptized ca 22 Jun 1755 at Sumiswald; 8 children:
    Verena, baptized 7 Jul 1777 at Rüegsau, Canton Bern, *married Christian Zuber.*
    Hans Ulrich, baptized 27 Dec 1778 at Rüegsau, *married Anna Winzenried.*
    Anna Barbara **Stalder**, baptized 30 Jul 1780 at Rüegsau, married to David (Jakob?) **Hausner (Housner)**.
    Samuel, born 1780.
    Anna, baptized 6 Oct 1782 at Rüegsau, *married C. Messerli.*
    Jakob, baptized 25 Mar 1786 at Rüegsau, *reportedly died 1812 in Moscow, Russia.*
    Magdalena, baptized 25 Jan 1789 at Eriswil, Canton Bern, reportedly married ca. May 1819 in Antwerp, United Netherlands (now Belgium), died in Athens County, OH, in the summer of 1824.[168]
    Ursula, born 4 Feb baptized 18 Feb 1792 at Rüegsau, married 1st ca. 1812 to
    Alois **Oberholzer, a miller.**
    Ursula was married 2nd on 24 Aug 1824 to:
        Fréderic Louis **Junod** born 18 Nov 1791 at Champ Favarger, Canton Neuchâtel, baptized 4 Dec 1791 at Liniéres, Canton Neuchâtel.
    Elisabeth, baptized 19 Oct 1794 at Rüegsau, married
Carl Friedrich **Gysi/Gysy/Guise/Guyse/Guysi**, born 17 Sep 1784 in Zofingen, Canton Aargau, went to Cincinnati/Avondale, Ohio, in 1826 and founded a German Society there.[169] Together with J. J. Märk and Adrian Rudolph Märk, he led a group of emigrants from Canton

---

[167] Shade, Nevin Mark, *The Stalder Home—Visited by Nevin M. Shade, 1975* (typescript, no location), 1-2.

[168] Schelbert and Rappolt, *Alles ist ganz anders hier*, 199.

[169] "Skizzen bekannter Pioniere: Carl Friedrich Guise. (Guyse.)," *Der deutsche Pionier*, (Cincinnati, Ohio, Der deutsche Pionier Verein von Cincinnati, ed. H[einrich] A[rmin] Rattermann), Vol. 4, Heft 7, 244.

Aargau to Amsterdam, where they arrived on 20 Mar 1817,[170] early enough to leave the harbor on the "La Babona," ahead of the ill-fated ship "Aprill," which suffered with hundreds of Aargauers losing their lives from illness in Texel and 73 from lack of provisions on board the passage.

Jacob **Stalder** was married 2nd on 7 Aug 1795 at Lützelflüh to
> Anna **Schweizer** of Hasle bei Burgdorf, Canton Bern, baptized either on 28 Feb 1773 or 12 Mar 1775 at Hasle. Children:
> *Christen, born on 18 Jun, baptized on 14 Jul 1797 at Belp, reportedly died in military service in Holland.*
> Catharina, born on 3 Feb, baptized on 23 Feb 1799 at Belp, reportedly married in New York in Aug 1819 to

Johannes **Finsterwald**, baptized 8 Jun 1788 at Stilli, Canton Aargau, Switzerland, son of Hans Finsterwald and his 3rd wife Barbara Wetter. Hans transported goods on ships between Zurich, Lucerne, Brugg, and Laufenburg, a typical occupation for men of Stilli, until his early death ca. 1795.[171] The son Johannes, possibly the group's poleman for the trip from Pittsburgh down the Ohio River judging by his common nickname "Captain," reportedly married Catharina Stalder in New York City after a courtship on board the ship. They lived among the German-speaking Swiss and Pennsylvanian settlers around Basil Township in Fairfield County, Ohio (a misspelling for Basel, now called Baltimore), until his early death ca. 1833, at which time widowed Catharina brought her children, the Finsterwalds, back to live among her Stalder relatives in the Swiss settlement in Athens County.[172]

> Rosina **Stalder**, born 5 Oct 1800, baptized 20 Feb 1801 at Belp, *married Jacob **Weis (Wyss)** on 12 Jun 1820.*

---

[170] "Vaterländische Nachrichten, Kanton Aargau. Schicksale einiger Auswanderer nach Amerika," *Der aufrichtige und wohlerfahrene Schweizer-Bote*, (Aarau: Heinrich Zschokke, 11 Dec 1817, No. 50), 393.

[171] E-mail from Max Baumann, Stilli, Canton Aargau, Switzerland, June 4, 2015.

[172] Charles H. Harris, "Finsterwalds Came to the Ohio Country With DeSteiguer Party From Switzerland," *The Harris History: A Collection of Tales of Long Ago of Southeastern Ohio and Adjoining Territories*, (Athens, Ohio: The Athens Messenger, 1957), 101-103.

Gysi.
Maria, baptized 23 Jun 1802 at Belp, *reportedly married a*
Friedrich, born 19 Sep, baptized 2 Oct 1803 at Belp, *married Marianna Lichti.*
Peter, baptized 23 Nov 1806 at Belp, *married Harriet B. Conner.*
Kaspar, born 24 Sep, baptized 8 Oct 1809 at Belp, *married Mary Ann Howard/Hauert.*
Niklaus, baptized 23 Feb 1812 at Rüegsau.
Andreas, baptized 29 Jun 1814 at Rüegsau.

Oswald **Marti/Martin**, born ca 1796, presumably in Bern, Canton Bern.

Christen **Mosimann**, possibly baptized either 7 Feb 1779 or 27 Oct 1782 at Sumiswald, Canton Bern, (married 7 Mar 1805 to Barbara Stalder)

John **Jenser**, born ca 1754, presumably in Bern.

Johann Jakob **Kocher**, possibly baptized either 11 Aug 1793 or 18 Aug 1798 in Büren an der Aare, Canton Bern.

Johann Jakob **Sut(t)er**, baptized 28 Feb 1796 in Büren an der Aare, Canton Bern.

Rudolph **Gribi**, baptized 5 May 1796 in Büren an der Aare, Canton Bern.

Johann Rudolph **Weibel**, of Büren an der Aare, Canton Bern, baptized 9 Apr 1789 in the Münster at Bern, and
Wife Anna **Kunz**, born ca 1795 in Meinisberg, Canton Bern
    John (Johann), born 11 Jul, baptized 21 Jul 1811 in Büren/Aare.
    Maria, born 25 Mar, baptized 11 Apr 1813 in Büren/Aare.
    Rudolph, born 15 Nov, baptized 27 Nov 1814 in Büren/Aare.

Franz **Lauden**, born ca 1798.
Maria, his wife, born ca 1800.

Bernhard **Walter**, born ca 1761 in Mühledorf, Canton Solothurn.

*Later joining the colony were Michael **Hubler**, baptized 16 Sep 1804 at Bätterkinden, Canton Bern, and his wife-to-be Elisabeth **Liechti**, baptized 14 Feb 1814.*

On the same ship was the family of the French-speaking commissioner, Jean Joseph **Labarthe**, who eventually went on to Louisiana:
Known in America as Jean (=John) Labarthe [of the Protestant family from Tonneins, Lot et Garonne, France],[173] baptized 27 Jan 1764 at Geneva, Switzerland, whom Gall describes as gray-haired, wearing yellow shoes, and holding a double-barreled shotgun.
Wife Jeanne Leonore/Eleonore **Chol(l)et**, baptized ca 1769 at Geneva, married 24 Jun 1792 in Geneva, died 1825 New Orleans, Louisiana
Three children died young, but four survived.
 Susanne, *born 18 Apr 1793 in Geneva, died 1793 in Geneva.*
 Joseph, *born 3 Apr 1794 in Geneva, died 25 Dec 1800 in Geneva.*
 Suzanne Marguerite, born 6 Mar 1795 in Geneva.
 Madeleine Josephine, *born 11 Mar 1796 in Geneva, died young.*
 Jean Joseph, born 2 Jul 1802 in Geneva, died 12 Jun 1874 in New Orleans, Louisiana, captain of the "Belle Isle," "A. W. Vanleer," "Rio Grande," "New Orleans," "Ceres," "Syndonia," "Governor Powell," and the "Flora," an Attakapas packet. During the Civil War he lost his ships and equipment, which were seized for Confederate service.
 François Philippe, born 1 Mar 1804 in Plainpalais, Geneva, a medical doctor in Assumption Parish, Louisiana.

---

[173] Derbes, Vincent J., *The Labarthe Family*, (New Orleans, LA: Vincent J. Derbes, 1986), 1.

Jean Auguste, born ca 29 Aug 1806 in Geneva, died 11 Nov 1869 in New Orleans, Louisiana.
More detail on this family is given elsewhere.

Also on the ship were:
Samuel Jean Pierre Daniel **R(e)ichenbach**, baptized 13 Dec 1774 at Lauenen, Canton Bern, a notary in Bern, the president of the emigration society, and his son
Albert August, born ca 1805.

Kinship bonds in the stem families were significant. If one is following only the male surname line, the role played by women can easily be overlooked. The beautiful Magdalena Stalder was the glue holding the Athens County colony together. Rudolph de Steiguer (born 1778) left Switzerland and crossed the ocean because of his love for her, and she was the common denominator between eight core Athens County families: Stalder (parents, siblings), de Steiguer (husband, stepchildren), Finsterwald (half-sister), Hausner (sister), Jewett (stepdaughter), Junod (sister), Oberholzer (sister), and Wyss (sister), as well as (stepdaughter) Uhl & Fahnestock in Wood County, Virginia (now West Virginia) and Washington County, Ohio.

Similarly, in the Monroe/Belmont group, Abraham Tüscher's wife Elisabetha Marti is Jakob Tüscher's daughter-in-law, a link with the Marti(n)s (daughter and sister) and she also has ties to the Fankhausers (as a baptismal sponsor), and following up that connection, the Fankhausers of Trub have ties to the Tschäppätts (a maternal grandmother). The four Fankhauser brothers account for the greatest number of descendants. The Tüscher immigrants, too, were quite prolific. Their settlement stimulated new waves of chain migration of Swiss friends and relatives, swelling especially to the riverfront areas of "dark Monroe" and Belmont Counties, with some overflow into Wetzel County, (West) Virginia. More than 200 Swiss surnames are recorded at one time or another in this community.

Later Swiss immigrants to this settlement include the Iseli/Isaly family, known for Isaly's ice cream stores and as the originators of Klondike® bars, including ancestors of the benefactor of the Ohio Genealogical Society's Samuel D. Isaly Library in Bellville, Ohio.

Though there was only a small, short-lived chain migration to the de Steiguer colony in Athens County and it did not prosper in the English-speaking environment, descendants have left their mark. One internationally-known descendant is Dow Finsterwald, 1958 PGA golf champion and Ryder Cup team member. Another was Rear Admiral Louis R. de Steiguer, Commander-in-Chief of the U.S. Battle fleet in 1927 and 1928.

Summing Up

How fragile our history is! Successful emigration often depends on timing. If the slightest event had not happened precisely as it did, we might not be here to study it. Had it not been for the magnificent ideas of the American Revolution in 1776 and the Northwest Ordinance, Napoleon's version of the French Revolution as applied to Switzerland in 1798, de Steiguer's and Tüscher's love affairs in the early 1800s, a volcano eruption halfway around the world in 1815, and the boldness and hardiness of the people themselves, not to mention the fact that the Ohio River was been at its lowest point in memory in 1819, plus countless other events, none of their thousands of descendants would have ever existed. If one of the three bullets from a Rhine toll collector at a new bridge between Ehrenbreitstein and Koblenz had killed Ludwig Gall or his boatman (I didn't even tell you about that narrow escape), if Gall had not found the horse in the dark that had run away with all the travel papers on its back, if an epidemic had broken out on the ships (as it did on the "Aprill" in Texel in the Netherlands in 1817, killing hundreds of Swiss from Canton Aargau), if the Prussian crackdown on Rhine travelers had occurred two weeks earlier, if the yellow fever epidemic had arrived in Philadelphia earlier, if the crazed passenger on the "*Eugénie*" had been able to carry out his threat to kill the captain—if, if, if—our story could easily have taken a terrible turn.

Descendants hear the happy-end histories told by the survivors, and the various victims along the way did not live to tell their tales. But the lives of the all Swiss pioneers of 1819 were actually hanging by a slim, delicate thread.

Acknowledgments:

Richard Acker, of the Summit County, Ohio, Chapter of the Ohio Genealogical Society, Akron, OH
Prof. Dr. Kurt Andermann, of the *Generallandesarchiv* in Karlsruhe, Baden, Germany
Vinzenz Bartlome, of the Swiss National Library, Bern, Switzerland
Max Baumann, historian, of Stilli, Canton Aargau, Switzerland
Melba Gorby Beard, descendant of Jakob Tüscher, deceased
Sarah Biäsch, of the Staatsarchiv of Canton Aargau
Thomas Bischof, civil registrar, Volketswil, Switzerland
Miriam Castagno, librarian, University of Bern, Bern, Switzerland
Reynold Chollet, family history researcher, Bottmingen, Switzerland
Wes Clarke, archaeologist of The Castle, Marietta, OH
Carey Clevenger, of the Parkersburg Wood County Public Library, Parkersburg, WV
Marion Coccejus, of the Hessian State Archive, Darmstadt, Germany
Janet Witten Conn, of the Wetzel County Public Library, New Martinsville, WV
Cristian Consuegra, student, history department, University of Bern, Bern, Switzerland
John Cunningham, of the Levering Library, Athens County Chapter of OGS, Athens, OH
Natalie de Bruyn, of the *Felixarchief*, Antwerp, Belgium
J. E. "Ed" de Steiguer, descendant of Baron von Steiger, of the University of Arizona, Tucson, AZ
Miriam Fankhauser, retired, Tiffin University, Tiffin, OH
Pierre-Yves Favez, Canton Vaud Archives, Chavannes-prés-Renens, Switzerland
Catherine Fedorchak, Monroe County, Ohio, genealogist, deceased
Joyce Fetty, of the Monroe County Public Library, Woodsfield, OH
Hubert Foerster, of the Fribourg Cantonal Archives, Fribourg, Switzerland
Eberhard Fritz, archivist of the Kingdom of Württemberg, Altshausen, Germany
Joseph Garrera, of the Lehigh Valley Historical Society, Allentown, PA

Peter Gsteiger, of the State Archive of Canton Bern, Switzerland
N. Hächler, civil registrar, Pieterlen, Canton Bern, Switzerland
Timm Harder, of the Evangelical church parish of Oberdiebach, Germany
Shirley A. Harmon, genealogist, Marietta, OH, who provided much assistance in searching Swiss records
Nina Hartmann, civil registrar's office, Volketswil, Switzerland
Thomas Hayoz, of the University of Bern Library, Bern, Switzerland
Jeff Herbert, records extractor and translator, Cincinnati, OH
Scott Holl, archivist at Eden Theological Seminary Archives, St. Louis, MO
Marguerite Abrigg Huffman, volunteer at Dally Memorial Library, Sardis, OH
Monika Hug, of the City and Technical University Library, Lucerne, Switzerland
Debbie Ice, editor, Friendly, WV
Jean-Jacques Jarrige, of the Seine-Maritime Department Archives, Rouen, France
Ronan Jehan, of the Defense Maritime History Archive, Brest, France
Jürg Kocher, archivist, Büren an der Aare, Canton Bern, Switzerland
Michael Lacopo, genealogist, Granger, IN
Vanessa Lange, of the Collegium Generale, University of Bern, Bern, Switzerland
Vincent Maroteaux, archivist of Départemental Archives of Seine-Maritime, Rouen, France
Karl F. Marbacher, genealogist, Lucerne, Switzerland
Lois Ann Mast, of *Mennonite Family History*, Morgantown, PA
Patricia McClure, technical writer/editor and French teacher, Charleston, WV
Tom McCullough, of the Moravian Archives, Bethlehem, PA
Dr. Andreas Metzing, archivist of the Evangelical Church Archive of the Rhineland, Boppard, Germany
Leander Meyer, of the library of the University of Bern, Bern, Switzerland
Jennifer Miller, of the Middlesex County College Library, Edison, NJ
Vic and Millie Mozena, Woodsfield, OH, of St. John's congregation, Powhatan Point, OH

Cheryl Ogden, of the Johnny Appleseed Education Center and Museum, Urbana, OH
John Ogden, of the Monroe County Historical Society and Chapter of OGS, Woodsfield, OH
Thomas O'Grady, of the Athens County Historical Society & Museum
Eva Ott, of the Municipal Archive, Biel, Switzerland
H.U. Pfister, archivist, Canton Zurich Archive, Zurich, Switzerland
Jeannette Rauschert, archivist of Canton Aargau Archive, Aarau, Switzerland
Bill Reynolds, historian at the Ohio River Museum, Ohio History Connection, Marietta, OH
Raoul Richner, city archivist of Aarau, Canton Aargau, Switzerland
Edward M. Rider, archivist of Nippert Collection, Cincinnati Historical Society, Cincinnati, OH
Franziska Rogger, archivist of the University of Bern, Bern, Switzerland
Judy G. Russell, The Legal Genealogist, genealogy blogger, Avenel, NJ
Jeanne Ruzchak-Eckman, genealogy blogger, of Pennsylvania
Cathy Sato, genealogical researcher, Powell, OH
Grace Schafer, deceased, descendant of Jacob Tüscher
W. Scheidegger-Brunner, civil registrar of Limpach, Switzerland
Leo Schelbert, of the University of Illinois at Chicago Circle, Chicago, IL
Helmut Schmahl, of the University of Mainz, Germany
Schönbucher, civil registrar of Meiringen, Switzerland
Marilyn Scott, Billy Ireland Cartoon Library & Museum, The Ohio State University, Columbus, OH
Linda Showalter, Special Collections librarian at the Marietta College Legacy Library, Marietta, OH
Tom Singer, historical docent, New Orleans, LA, who provided much research on Louisiana families
Fritz Stalder, attorney, former member of *Heiliggeist* Church council, Bern, Switzerland
Barbara Studer Immenhauser, archivist of Canton Bern Archive, Bern, Switzerland
Ray Swick, retired historian of the Blennerhassett Island Historical Park, Parkersburg, WV

Carol Swinehart, genealogist, Lancaster, OH
Dr. Frank Teske, archivist of the municipal archive of Mainz, Germany
Danny Teurelincx, of the municipal archive of Antwerp, Belgium
Tobias Teyke, archivist of the municipal archive of Trier, Germany
Charles Tisher, deceased, descendant of Jakob Tüscher, and wife Marjorie, deceased, Salt Lake City, UT
Lester John Tisher, descendant of Jakob Tüscher, Bellingham, WA, deceased
Don Heinrich Tolzmann, German-American author, Cincinnati, OH
Alexandra Tschakert, of the State Archive of Basel-Stadt, Switzerland
Benno von Däniken, civil registrar of Wangen an der Aare, Switzerland
Johanna Vonnez, civil registrar of Payerne, Switzerland
Karine Weber, of *Archives Départementales du Bas-Rhin*, Strasbourg, France
Christelle Wick, archivist of Toggenburger Museum, Lichtensteig, Switzerland
Amanda Winkler, of the *Gemeindeschreiberei*, Fraubrunnen, Switzerland
Rachel Wintemberg, The Helpful Art Teacher, Perth Amboy, NJ
Denise Wittwer, of the *Burgerbibliothek*, Bern, Switzerland

État nominatif des émigrants Suisses et
Allemands qui sont à Anvers s'embarquant à
bord du navire français L'Eugénie pour le Nouveau monde

Nom	Prénom	Âge	Domicile	Observations
Gall	Louis	28	Troyes	
Willwersch	Marie	18	id	Sans épouse
Gall	Martin	64	id	
"	Marg.te	64	id	Sans épouse
Boldt	G.me	34	Solingen	
Lickel	Fried.g.me	18	id	
Feldskien	Christian	20	Weimar	
Uschard	Nicolas	19	Hamburg	
Kuhl	Henry	19	id	
Guil	Henry	19	id	
Kuhl	Philippe	20	id	
Dallenkopf	Jean	25	Pfaffingen	
Dubois	Daniel	40	Liège	
"	Adèle	35	id	
"	Auguste	13	id	
"	Eugénie	4	id	
Lindenlist	J.	29	Anvers	
Plitschie	Martin	66	Schaffhouse	
"	Elisabeth	66	id	Sans épouse
"	Ferenne	30	id	
"	André	21	Asbach	
"	Pierre	20	id	
"	Virginie	18	Metzgrits	

24	Gerret	Jacques	18	Unterrietsheim
25	Neuffer	Chrétien	2	Horkheim
26	Gravenstein	Catharina	22	Lachy...
27	Neuffer	Christine	2	Lochgau
28	Buck	Jean	20	Obergimbach
29	Muller	J. Geo.	30	Schoray
30	Schaeffer	Margt.	30	d°
31	Muller	Christ.	5	d°
32	d°	Frederick	1	d°
33	d°	Catharina	20	d°
34	Nonnenmacher	J. Geo.	18	d°
35	Zoll	J. Geo.	15	d°
36	Meiterinn	Barbe	35	Heinzheim
37	Zoll	Elisa	18	Schoray
38	d°	J. Geo.	10	d°
39	d°	Frederick	4½	d°
40	Kubach	J. Geo.	43	Unterrietsheim
41	Heidelein	Regine	22	d°
42	Frankhauser	Dan.l	34	Trub
43	d°	Marie	25	d°
44	d°	Dan.l	6	d°
45	d°	Jean	4	d°
46	d°	Madeleine	2	d°
47	Spialet	Sophie	21	Ibam
48	Frankhauser	Nicolas	38	Trub
49	d°	Nicolas	18	d°
50	d°	David	12	d°
51	d°	Susanne	11	d°
52	d°	Jnverena	9	d°

Frankhauser	Jarinote	70	Eriz	
d°	ure mario	8	d°	
d°	Jean	3	d°	
d°	Cath.	1	d°	
Butcher	J^n	43	Conersinhof	
d°	Catha	29	d°	Laf auma
d°	Jean	10	d°	
d°	y gne	8	d°	
d°	anne	7	d°	
d°	N°		d°	
d°	Marie	3	d°	
d°	Abraham	22	d°	
d°	Elise	25	d°	
d°	y gne	1	d°	
d°	Elizab.	6	d°	
Morle	J^n	71	Halfhie	
d°	Jean	31	d°	
d°	Christin	22	d°	
Huggi	Benoit	58	Jumsswald	
d°	marie	36	d°	
d°	Samuel	11	d°	
d°	Christin	8	d°	
d°	Benoit	6	d°	
d°	Rudolph	1	d°	
Dams	J^n	27	Anvers	
Flallser	"	22	d°	
Schopp		36	Gelzingen	
d°		15	d°	
d°		13	d°	
d°	Cath.	11	d°	

83	Tchappat	J.ᵖʳᵉ	9	Galzinger
84	id	Mᵉ anne	6	id
85	id	Friedᶜʰ	2	id
86	Schneider	Denise	42	Bronzenhof
87	id	Barbe	29	id
88	id	Sigᵉ	16	id
89	id	Eliza	8	id
90	id	Benoit	6	id
91	id	Madᵉ	2	id
92	id	Jean		id
93	Schmidt	Louis	26	Burg
94	Stamm	Martin	62	Schaffrouse
95	id	Marlene	35	id
96	id	Jean	9	id
97	id	Louis	6	id
98	id	Christine	2	id
99	id	Verena	11	id
100	id	Madeleine	7	id
101	Spitler	François	69	Berne
102	Stamm	Madeleine	28	Berne
103	Deeden	Lᵗ Augᵗ	61	id
104	Mespelter	Jeanne	72	Bruxelles
105	Cornet	Geoffr	33	Anvers

Neuss le 22 Mai 1819

pour copie conforme
Jullien

Certifié conforme le présent
état nominatif des passagers
montant à cent cinq personnes
en tout

Neuss 24 Mai 1819
Jullien

[Handwritten list, largely illegible. Partial reading:]

[heading, two lines — illegible]

#	Name	Age		
1				
2				
3			80	
4			17	
5	B...	16		
6	Bartell	10		
7	~~illegible~~	36		Nelsey Meyer
8	Albert August	18		
9	John Lebart..	35	General	Trader
10		38		
11		22		
12	John Joseph	16		
13	Pierre ...	15		
14	Au...	13		
15	~~illegible~~	24		...Neigh...
16	~~illegible~~	23		do
17	Jacob ...	62	...ffth	Farmer
18	...	60		
19	Fred...	13		
20	Peter	13		
21	Casper	11		
22	Nicolas	9		
23	...			
24	Charlott			
25	Cather...	19		
26	...	10		
27	Jacob ...	30	Born	farmer
28	... Chas...	32		...Meier
29	...la	25		
30	...	4		

31	David Neusser	30	Berne	farmer
32	Barbara	"	38	"
33	Elisabeth	"	16	"
34	Maria	"	13	"
35	Anna	"	9	"
36	Hans Eberhard	31	Graubünd	Taylor
37	Anna	"	25	"
38	~~Lewis Laborn~~	32	"	Servant Negro
39	Oswald Martin	33	Berne	Taylor
40	Anna	"	35	"
41	Eliza Neusser	50	"	Butcher
42	Christian Mussigman	46	Summerset	Weaver
43	Jacob Hocker	35	Berne	Potter
44	Jacob Butler	23	"	Taylor
45	Rudolph Graß	28	"	Sadler
46	Jacob Weiß	19	Berne	do
47	Rudolph Bibl	50	Berne	Farmer
48	Anna	"	40	"
49	John	"	10	"
50	Napolon	"	8	"
51	Maria	"	6	"
52	Mathias Heusler	31	"	Shoemaker
53	Nicolas	"	21	"	do
54	~~Lawrent Gütli~~	53	"	Vintner Negro
55	~~Andrew Groß~~	19	Leuthern	Painter
56	~~Truit Lenn~~	"	Berne	Taylor
57	~~Mario~~	"	9	"
58	Bernard Walter	58	Michendof	farmer
59	Charles Prince	"	Nesplat	Sadler

[MASTER'S OATH ON ENTERING VESSEL.]

I _____ do solemnly, sincerely, and truly _____ that the report and manifest, subscribed with my name, and now delivered by me to the Collector of the District of New-York, contains, to the best of my knowledge and belief, a just and true account of all the goods, wares and merchandise, including packages of every kind and nature whatsoever, which were on board the _____ at the time of her sailing from the port of _____ or which have been laden or taken on board at any time since; and that the packages of the said goods are as particularly described as in the bills of lading; signed for the same by me, or with my knowledge; that I am at present, and have been during the voyage, master of the said vessel—that no package whatsoever, or any goods, wares, or merchandise, have been unladen, landed, taken out, or in any manner whatever removed from on board the said _____ since her departure from the said port of _____ (except such as are now particularly specified and declared in the abstract account herewith) and that the clearance and other papers, now delivered by me to the Collector, are all that I now have, or have had, that any way relate to the cargo of the said vessel. And I do further _____ that the several articles specified in the said manifest, as the sea-stores for the cabin and vessel, are truly such, and were bona fide put on board the said _____ for the use of the officers, crew and passengers thereof, and have none of them been brought, and are not intended, by way of merchandise, or for sale, or for any other purpose than above mentioned, and are intended to remain on board for the consumption of the said officers and crew. I further _____ that if I shall hereafter discover, or know of any other, or greater quantity of goods, wares and merchandise, of any nature or kind whatsoever, than are contained in the report and manifest subscribed and now delivered by me, I will immediately, and without delay, make due report thereof to the Collector of the Port or District of New-York. And I do likewise _____ that all matters whatsoever in the said report and manifest expressed, are, to the best of my knowledge, just and true. I further _____ that _____ officer of the customs has applied for an inspection of the manifest of the cargo on board the said vessel, and that _____ certificate of indorsement has been delivered to me on _____ manifest of such cargo.

So help me God.

_____ to this _____

Before me _____ _____ Collector.

A. W. Vanleer, boat	97	Baisch	42	
Aachen, Rhineland, Germany	11	Baker, Jim	51	
Aarau, Canton Aargau	89, 90	Baltimore, Fairfield County, Ohio		95
Aare River	21, 37	Balz, Anna Barbara	92	
Aargau, canton	21, 29, 62, 89, 94, 99	Barber family	ii	
		Barber, Levi	38	
Abel's Cheese	55	Bare, Jacob	32	
Äberhardt, Louise	77	Baresville, Ohio	32	
Adair, John	40	Baron von Steiger...see Steiger		
Adams, John Quincy	ii, 14	Basel, Switzerland	34, 47, 58	
Adkins, Andrea	48	Basil, Fairfield County, Ohio	58, 95	
Admittance, ship	42	Bätterkinden, Canton Bern	97	
Aeberhard...see also Eberhard		Bauer, Catharina	84	
Aeberhard, Johannes Adam	81, 89	Baumberger, Jakob	53	
Aeschbacher, Jacob	89	Baumgartner, Barbara	29, 88	
Aeschlimann family	54	Bavaria	21	
Aetna, boat	43	Bayou Teche, Louisiana	19	
Affoltern, Canton Bern	93	Beard, Melba (Gorby)	6	
Agin, France, diocese	20	Beatnell, P.	35	
Aix-la-Chapelle...see Aachen		Bedford, Pennsylvania	29, 36	
Albrecht, J.G.	42	Belgium	44, 74	
Aldenhoven	12	Belle Isle, boat	97	
Allendrelle la Malmaison, France	74	Bellevue, villa	44	
Allentown, Pennsylvania	30	Bellona, boat	43	
Alpina, colony, New York	58	Bellville, Ohio	98	
Alsace	21, 34, 53	Belmont County, Ohio	30, 52, 65, 66, 82, 89, 98	
Ames family	ii			
Ames, Edward, Bishop	57	Belp, Canton Bern	94, 95	
Ames, Laura Watson	57	Belpre, Ohio	39	
Ames Township, Athens County	38	Berlin, Germany	37, 39	
Amsterdam, Netherlands	13, 21, 63, 79, 80, 81, 94	Bern, Switzerland	1, 2, 5, 7, 8, 9, 11, 15, 17, 21, 34, 37, 40, 46, 47, 53, 57, 59, 60, 73, 77, 78, 82, 85, 86, 87, 91, 92, 93, 95, 96, 97	
Antenen, Jacob	29			
Antwerp (now Belgium)	13, 24, 25, 34, 42, 44, 60, 61, 67, 68, 69, 72, 73, 74, 76, 79, 80, 81, 82, 83, 84, 88, 89, 94	Berne...see Bern		
		Best, Carl C.	52	
		Best, Charles Carroll	52	
Antwerpen...see Antwerp		Bethel Church	51	
Anvers...see Antwerp		Bethlehem, Pennsylvania	28, 29	
Apostolic Christian Church, Sardis, Ohio	53, 64	Bethlehem, Stark County, Ohio	91	
		Biehl, Philipp	44	
Aprill, ship	21, 62, 67, 94, 99	Biel, Canton Bern	88	
		Bienne...see Biel		
Arkansas	66	Big Buckeye	33	
Arkansas Post	41	Bilder, Mary Sarah	45	
Arkansas River	41	Bimeler	42	
Arkansas Territory	ii, 41	Binger Loch (Rhine narrows)	22	
Arn, Elisabeth	9, 47, 84	Black Horse Inn, Pennsylvania	43	
Arn, Maria	84	Blackburn, Samuel	40	
Ascension Parish, Louisiana	20, 41	Blennerhassett, Harman	ii, 39	
Assumption Parish, Louisiana	20, 97	Blennerhassett Island	39	
Athens, Ohio	57, 58, 59	Blunier, Elisabeth	54	
Athens County, Ohio	65, 66, 93, 94, 95, 97, 98	Bogilboden (Buckhill Bottom)	64	
		Bolligen, Canton Bern	87	
Atlantic Ocean	35	Bonaparte, Joseph	ii, 43	
Attakapas, Louisiana	97	Bonaparte, Napoleon	ii, 9, 43, 56, 99	
Attert, Belgium	74	Bonn, Washington County, Ohio		51
Auf der Feldmatt	90	Bonnhorst, Charles von	41	
Auf Ryffersegg	90, 91	Boone, Daniel	ii, 30	
Austro-Hungarian Empire	13	Bordentown, New Jersey	43	
Avondale, Ohio	94	Boston, Massachusetts	35	
Baden, Germany	10, 21, 34	Boudry, Canton Neuchâtel	58	

Boujean...see Bözingen	
Bözingen, Canton Bern	73, 74, 88
Brazil	ii, 5, 17
Bremgarten, Canton Bern	91
Brest, France	25, 67, 83
Bretten, Baden	93
Brooklyn, New York	65
Brossy, Abram	85
Brossy, Jeanne Marie	83, 84
Brossy, Maria	7
Bruen, Matthias	27, 30, 63
Brug	73, 74
Bruges, Belgium	74
Brügg, Canton Bern	74
Brugg, Canton Aargau	54, 95
Brugge, Belgium	74
Brunell, F. & A.	35
Brunnadern, Bern	91
Brunner, Otto	54
Brussels, Belgium	73, 74
Bruxelles...see Brussels	
Bubendorf, Canton Basel-Landschaft	54
Buchberg, Canton Schaffhausen	54
Bucher, Jacob	65
Buck, Jean	70
Buck, Johann	70
Buckhill Bottom, Ohio	64
Bure...see Büren an der Aare	
Burenzumhof...see Büren zum Hof	
Büren an der Aare, Canton Bern	7, 77, 78, 89, 95, 96
Büren zum Hof, Canton Bern	6, 7, 71, 72, 74, 79, 80, 83, 86, 89
Burgenthal, Anna Louise	87
Burkholder, Hans	17
Burr, Aaron	2, 39
Bury, Dr. Joseph	58
Bussy-Chardonnary, Canton Vaud	88
Byron, (Lord)	ii, 10
Cain Ridge, Monroe County, Ohio	52
Calvin, John	19
Campus Martius, Marietta, Ohio	93
Canaan Township, Athens County	38
Captina Creek, Ohio	32, 64
Captina, Ohio	30
Ceres, boat	97
Chambersburg, Pennsylvania	37
Champ Favarger, Canton Neuchâtel	94
Châtelard	15
Chicago, Illinois	30
Chief Cornstalk	ii, 30
Chillon	10
Cholet...see Chollet	
Chollet, Jeanne Eleonore	19, 97
Cincinnati, Ohio	30, 44, 49, 54, 65, 94
Clarington, Ohio	52, 55
Cleveland, James	30
Collot, Victor	31
Columbia, ship	35, 36, 40, 67, 76, 83
Conestoga Inn	43
Congress of Vienna	2
Conner, Harriet B.	95
Conseil, Lt. Jules Aimé	26
Cornet, Joseph	44, 73
Cornett, G.me Jos.h	73
Cornstalk...see Chief Cornstalk	
Cramer, Zadock	ii, 30, 38
Cronau, Rudolf	37, 39
Cumberland Presbyterian Church, Athens, Ohio	57
Cypress Grove Cemetery, New Orleans, Louisiana	20
D'Arcy Wood, Gillen	3
Dairy, Monroe County, Ohio	54
Dams, J.ques	72
de Büren, Friedrich	59, 93
De Caen, L.uis Aug.te	45, 73
de Graffenried...see Graffenried	
de Groot, Capt. Dirk Cornelisz	62
de Steiguer...see also Steiger	9, 66, 98
de Steiguer, Alexandra	9
de Steiguer, Louis Philippe	59
de Steiguer, Louis R., Admiral	98
de Steiguer, Rodolphe, Jr.	57
de Vasserot..see Wasserroth	
DeForest, Capt. John	27
Delar, Henry	76
Delaware	62
Delaware River	42, 43
Delpeche, Andrew	77
"Deutschheim"	44
DeWitt, Dr.	36
Diamond, J.	35
Donaldsonville, Louisiana	20
Downingtown, Pennsylvania	36, 43
Dordrecht	34
Douanne...see Twann	
Dover, England	45
Dubach, Rosina	85
Duffy, Ohio	54
Duffy Run, Monroe County, Ohio	54
DuFour, Jacques	14
DuFour, Jean François	14
Durand, M.	35
Dürrenroth, Canton Bern	54
Dutch East Indies	3
Easton, Pennsylvania	29
Eberhard, Adam	77, 81, 89
Eberhard, Anna	77
Eberhard, Nicolas...see Eberhar(d)t	
Eberhar(d)t, Niklaus	6, 44, 69, 89
Eggleston, Edward	50
Ehrenbreitstein, Germany	99
Elie, Anaise	19
Elsass...see Alsace	
Emma, ship	42
Emmental region, Canton Bern	54
English Channel	45
Erie Canal	65
Eriswil, Canton Bern	94

Ernst, Ferdinand	16	Finsterwald, Jacob	77
Eugénie, ship	23, 24, 25, 41, 62, 63, 67, 68, 83, 85, 87, 99	Finsterwald, Johannes	95
		Finsterwald, John	37
Everett, Edward	ii, 15, 61	Finsterwald family	66, 98
Fahnestock, Obed	65	Fisching Krik...see Fishing Creek	
Fahnestock, William	93	Fishing Creek, Monroe County Ohio	91
Fahnestock family	98	Flora, boat	97
Fairfield County, Ohio	58, 95	Flourtown, Pennsylvania	43
Fankhauser, Anna	92	Fraitas, Louisa M.	19
Fankhauser, Anna Maria	86	France	1, 13, 18, 19, 62, 63, 65, 67
Fankhauser, Anne Marie	71		
Fankhauser, Carl Ludwig	86	Frankhauser...see Fankhauser	
Fankhauser, Cath.e	71	Franklin, Benjamin	ii, 28
Fankhauser, Catharina	91	Franklin, Williams	28
Fankhauser, Christian	92	Franklin House hotel	65
Fankhauser, Daniel	29, 70, 82, 85, 91	Frauenarbeitshaus, Bern	85
		Fraubrunnen, Canton Bern	47, 79, 84
Fankhauser, Daniel jr.	30, 70	French Five Hundred	ii, 30
Fankhauser, Elisabetha	82, 92	French Revolution	2, 15
Fankhauser, Friedrich	92	Friedrichsdorf, Hessen	49
Fankhauser, G.me	71	Frillon	73
Fankhauser, J.n Arnold	71	Fröhlich, Samuel Heinrich	54
Fankhauser, J.n Werner	71	Frommern, Württemberg	42
Fankhauser, Jacob Eugen Ocean	62, 82, 87	Frost, Robert	7
		Frutigen	29
Fankhauser, Jean	71	Fürstenwärther, Moritz von	15, 25, 57, 63
Fankhauser, Johann Samuel Arnold "Andy"	86	Gagern, Hans Christoph Ernst von	14, 16, 62
Fankhauser, Johann Werner	86	Gall, Franz Peter	12
Fankhauser, Johannes	70, 87, 91	Gall, Louis...see Gall, Ludwig	
Fankhauser, Louis	71	Gall, Ludwig	I, 12, 13, 14, 15, 16, 17, 22, 23, 24, 25, 27, 40. 41, 42, 43, 45, 57, 60, 61, 62, 63, 65, 66, 68, 74, 75, 97, 99
Fankhauser, Ludwig	71		
Fankhauser, Madelaine	71		
Fankhauser, Magdalena	71, 87	Gall, Marg.te	68
Fankhauser, Maria	92	Gall, Maria Anna	41
Fankhauser, Maria Catharina	86	Gall, Martin	68
Fankhauser, Maria Elisabeth	92	Gallatin, Albert	ii, 16, 33
Fankhauser, Marie	70	Gallipolis, Ohio	ii, 30
Fankhauser, Miriam	33	Gehring family	54
Fankhauser, Nicolas	71	Gehring, Isaac	54
Fankhauser, Nicolas jr.	71	Geit, Thierry...see Heit	
Fankhauser, Niklaus	22, 29, 32, 33, 63, 70, 82, 85, 86, 91, 92	General Washington Inn, Pennsylvania	43
		Geneva, Switzerland	15, 16, 19, 20, 33, 40, 41, 77, 97
Fankhauser, Niklaus jr.	70, 86		
Fankhauser, Rudolf Wilhelm	86	Genf...see Geneva	
Fankhauser, Samuel	91, 92	Gerber family	54
Fankhauser, Samuel jr.	92	Gerber, Rosina	87
Fankhauser, Susanna Maria	86	Gerock, Jacques	69
Fankhauser, Susanne	71	Gerock, Jakob	69
Fankhauser, Wilhelm	71	Glanzmann, Anna	89
Fankhauser family	64, 87, 98	Glanzmann, Anna Barbara	89
Fankhouser ...see Fankhauser		Gleim, Christian	65
Fanshe, William	93	Goetz, George	31
Fearing family	ii	Gonen, J.	35
Fearing, Paul	38	Gotzingen...see Bözingen	
Federal Creek	38	Governor Powell, boat	97
Feldmatt, Röthenbach	90	Graf(f)enried, Canton Bern	77, 78, 81, 88, 89
Feller, Maria	87		
Finsterwald, "Captain"	95	Graffenried, von, family	10
Finsterwald, Dow	98	Gravenried...see Graffenried	
Finsterwald, Hans	95	Gran(d)son, Canton Vaud	10

Granger, Agin, France	20		Hof Lehn, Rüegsbach, Canton Bern	93
Grauer, B.	35		Holland	34, 95
Grauholz, Battle of, Bern	1, 6		Holmes County, Ohio	53, 92
Gravenried...see Graffenried			Holy Ghost Church, Bern	85
Gravenstein, Catherine	70		Horkheim, Württemberg	69
Great Kanawha River	30, 64		Houbar, Adéle	69
Gribi, Louis	78		Houbar, Aug.te	69
Gribi, Ludwig	78		Houbar, Daniel	44, 69
Gribi, Rudolph	78, 97		Houbar, Eugénie	69
Gribi family	78		Housner...see Hausner	
Grüningen, John Paul von	46		Howard, Arnold	59, 60
Grüterhof, Canton Bern	93		Howard, Mary Ann	96
Guise...see Gysi			Howe, Henry	ii
Guyse...see Gysi			Howland, GG & S	35
Guysi...se Gysi			Hubler, Michael	97
Gygli, Yvonne	46		Huggi...see Hugi	
Gysi, --	95		Hugi, Bendicht	72, 88
Gysi, Carl Friedrich	94		Hugi, Bendicht jr.	72, 88
Gysy...see Gysi			Hugi, Benoit	72
Haller, Albrecht von	ii, 9		Hugi, Benoit jr.	72
Hannibal, Ohio	32		Hugi, Chrétien	72, 88
Hannover	17		Hugi, Christen	88
Hanover	17		Hugi, Maria	82
Hardie, Charles L.	19		Hugi, Maria jr.	88
Harmar, Washington County, Ohio		93	Hugi, Marie	72
Harmonie Gesellschaft	42, 85		Hugi, Rudolf	88
Harmony Society	42, 85		Hugi, Rudolph	72
Harrisburg, Pennsylvania	36, 44, 45, 65, 66		Hugi, Samuel	72, 88
			Hügli, Anna	94
Harrisville, New York	58		Illinois	ii, 14, 15, 18
Hasle bei Burgdorf, Canton Bern		89, 95	Illman & Sons	29
			Ilsfeld, Württemberg	74
Hässig, Margaretha	90		Im Hilchli, Canton Bern	90
Hässig, Rosina	90		In den Erlen, Canton Bern	87
Hauert...see also Howard			Indiana	ii 14, 36, 66
Hauert, Arnold	59		Indonesia	3
Hauert, Joseph	59		Iowa	87
Hauert, Mary Ann	96		Isaly, Samuel D.	98
Hausner, Anna	77		Isaly family	98
Hausner, Barbara	77		Iseli family	98
Hausner, David	77, 94		Ittigen, Canton Bern	87
Hausner, Elisabeth	77		Jallan	73
Hausner, Maria	77		Jallou	73
Hausner family	66, 98		Jenner, von	10
Heckel, Fréd G.me	68		Jenser, John	78, 96
Heckel, Friedrich Wilhelm	68		Jewett, Leonidas	93
Heilbronn, Württemberg	16		Jewett family	ii, 98
Heiliggeistkirche, church, Bern	85		Johlingen, Germany	74
Heinsheim, Baden	70		Jöhlingen, Germany	74
Heischlin, Régine	70		Jones, Capt. John Paul	38
Heisely, George	65		Jullan	73
Heisley, George	65		Jullon	73
Heit, Theodor	44, 69		Jullou, Capt. François Jean Allain	26, 63, 67, 73, 84, 88, 89
Helvetic Republic	1, 56			
Henderson, New York	57		Jullow	73
Herzogenbuchsee, Canton Bern	89		Jung, André	69
Hessen	21, 44, 49		Jung, Andreas	44, 69
Hetuck (Sproat)	32		Junod, Elisabeth	94
Hicks, Benjamin	76		Junod, Fréderic Louis	94
Hilchli, Canton Bern	90		Junod family	66, 98
Hilltop Swiss Lads and Laddies	55		Jura region, Switzerland	17

Kanawha River	30, 31		Labarthe, Marie Clara	20
Käptin (Captina), Ohio	64		Labarthe, Paulene Eleonore	20
Karl Friedrich, Grand Duke of Baden	10, 92		Labarthe, Philippe (2)	20
			Labarthe, Philippe A.	19
Karlsruhe, Baden	10, 92		Labarthe, Pierre	18
Keiser, Mathias	78		Labarthe, Susan Margaret	77
Keller, Johannes	55		Labarthe, Susanne	97
Kentucky	14, 40		Labarthe, Suzanne Marguerite	19, 767 97
Keokuk, Iowa	87		Labarthe, Therese Emelie	20
Key, Francis Scott	65		Lâd(e)rach, Barbara	86
Kidron, Ohio	17		Laich, C.	42
Kilchhofer, David	17		Lake Geneva	9, 37
Kirchberg, Canton Bern	88, 89		Lake Lucerne	37
Kirchdorf, Canton Bern	86, 87		Lake Neuchatel	37
Kirchthurnen, Canton Bern	87		Lake Thun	37
Kirkpatrick, Rachel	86		Lake Zurich	37
Kleeburger Hof, estate	14		Lancaster, Pennsylvania	36, 44
Koblenz, Germany	99		Landolf, Jakob	6
Kocher family	78		Landry, Marie Delzine	19
Kocher, Jacob	78		Langnau, Canton Bern	82
Kocher, Johann Jakob	96		LaSagne, Canton Neuchâtel	83
Koertz, Barbara	86		Lau, cabinetmaker	34
Köniz, Canton Bern	92		Lauden, Franz	96
Kopp, J.n George	69		Lauden, Maria	96
Krumbhaar, Louis	40, 41		Lauenen, Canton Bern	97
Kubach, J. J.ques	70		Laufenburg, Canton Aargau	95
Kubach, Johann Jakob	70		Lausanne, Canton Vaud	93
Kugler, I.	35		LeHavre, France	9, 25, 82, 90
Kuhl, Heinrich	44, 69		Lebanon, Pennsylvania	29
Kuhl, Henry...see Kuhl, Heinrich			Lehmann, Emil	i
Kunz, Anna	97		Lehmann, Peter	17
Küpfer, Ludwig	15		Lehmann, Ulrich	17
Kur(t)z, Capt. Daniel L.	34, 67, 76, 78		Leipzig, Saxony	41
Kuster, Mathias	78		Leopold, Friedrich Wilhelm	65
Kuster, Nicolas	78		Lewis County, New York	58
L--, Francis	78		Lichtensteig, Canton St. Gallen	4
L--, Maria	78		Lichti, Marianna	97
La Babona, ship	94		Liebeskind, Chrètien	68
Labathe, August	77		Liebeskind, Christian	44, 68
Labarthe, Delphine	19		Liechti, Elisabeth	97
Labarthe, Ernest Leonard	19		Liechti...see also Lichti	
Labarthe, Felicien Adele	20		Liége, Belgium	44, 69
Labarthe, Francis Philipp	77		Lignières, Canton Neuchâtel	94
Labarthe, François Philippe	20, 76, 97		Limpach, Canton Bern	9, 83, 85, 89
Labarthe, Jean Alphonse	20		Little Captina Creek	40
Labarthe, Jean Auguste	19, 20, 76, 97		Little Miami River	66
Labarthe, Jean Etienne	20		Liverpool, England	76, 78
Labarthe, Jean Joseph	16, 18, 19, 33, 40, 41, 66, 76, 97		Locarno, Canton Tessin	90
			Löchgau, Württemberg	73, 74
Labarthe, Jean Joseph Jr.	19, 76, 97		Lochmann, Georg	65
Labarthe, Joanna Leonore	76		Lockgau, Germany	69, 74
Labarthe, John Alexander	19		Lonkgau, Germany	70, 74
Labarthe, John Joseph	19, 77		Lord Byron	9
Labarthe, Joseph	97		Lorelei, rock along Rhine	22
Labarthe, Joseph Numa	20		Lot et Garonne, France	18, 97
Labarthe, Louise Caroline	19		Louisiana	2, 17, 19, 41, 66, 97, 97
Labarthe, Madeleine Josephine	97			
Labarthe, Marguerite Alice	20		Louisville, Kentucky	40
Labarthe, Marie Aglee	20		Lowrie, Walter	40
Labarthe, Marie Laura	20		Lucas, Francisca	90
Labarthe, Marie Louise Claire	19		Lucerne, Switzerland	95

Lüsslingen, Canton Solothurn	54	Mississippi River	41, 65
Lüterkofen, Canton Solothurn	54	Missouri	ii, 93
Luzelfluh...see Lützelflüh		Missouri River	65
Lützelflüh, Canton Bern	77, 78, 93, 95	Moers, Marg.te	68
Machern, Johann	44	Mollenkopf, Jean	44, 69
Magdeburg, Saxony	89	Mollenkopf, Johann	44, 69
Maibach, Margaretha	54	Mömbris-Rappach, Bavaria	44, 69, 74
Maienknecht, Jacob	85	Monroe County, Ohio	32, 52, 53, 59, 65, 66, 82, 89, 90, 91, 98
Maienknecht, Philippine	84		
Main River	21	Monroe Mission	51, 52
Mainz, Germany	21	Montgomery & Sons	35
Malmaison, France	74	Moravian Seminary	29
Marburg, Hessen	69	Moscow, Russia	94
Marietta, Ohio	39, 51, 66, 91, 93	Moselle river	13
		Moser, Barbara	90
Märk, Adrian Rudolph	94	Mosimann, Christian	78, 96
Märk, J. J.	94	Mossimann...see Mosimann	
Marshall County, (West) Virginia	65	Mühledorf, Canton Solothurn	78, 96
Marti, Chrétien	72, 80, 88, 90	Mühlheim...see Mülchi	
Marti, Christen	72, 80, 88, 90	Mülchi, Canton Bern	7, 72, 74, 80, 84, 85, 87
Marti, Elise (m Tüscher)	71, 85, 88, 98		
Marti, Elisabeth (m Tüscher)	72, 85, 88, 98	Mulchie...see Mülchi	
Marti, Elisabeth	87	Muller, Catharine	70
Marti, J.ques	47, 72, 80, 87, 88	Muller, Chrêt.	70
		Müller, Christian	70
Marti, Jacob	47, 72, 80, 87, 88	Müller, Ernst	47
		Muller, Frederick	70
Marti, Jacob iii	88	Müller, Friedrich	70
Marti, Jacob jr.	87, 91	Muller, J.J.ques	70
Marti, Jakob	80	Müller, Johann Jakob	69
Marti, Jean	72, 80, 88	Müller, Maria Louise Wilhelmine	92
Marti, Johann(es)	72, 80, 88	Müller, Wilhelmine	10, 92
Marti family	64, 98	Muri, Canton Bern	86, 91
Martin...see also Marti		Murray, Magnus Miller	40
Martin family	64, 98	Mürset(h), Maria Elisabeth	86
Martin, Aglee	20	Müslin, David, Rev.	57
Martin, Anna	78	Muster, Elisabeth	93
Martin, Joseph Richard	20	Naples, Italy	43
Martin, Oswald	77, 96	Napoleon...see Bonaparte	
Maryland	48	Nast, Wilhelm	49, 51
Marx, Karl	60	National Road	29
Maximilian, Prince of Wied-Neuwied	41	Nautilus, boat,	27, 43
May, Emanuel Gabriel	10	Netherlands	99
McCrea & Slidell	35	Neuchâtel	10, 78
McLaughlin, Capt.	42	Neuchâtel, canton	58, 78, 83, 87
Mediterranean Sea	42	Neufchatel	78
Meinisberg, Canton Bern	97	Neuffer, Chrétien	69, 70
Meiringen, Canton Bern	84	Neuffer, Christian	69, 70
Mespelter, Jeanne	73	Neuffer, Christine	69
Messen, Canton Bern (now Canton Solothurn) 80, 85, 87		Neumatt, Trub, Canton Bern	54
		New Bern, North Carolina	9
Messerli, C.	94	New Brunswick, New Jersey	43
Messerli, Jakob	6	New Orleans, Louisiana	19, 20, 97
Messmer, Beat Ludwig	15	New Castle, Delaware	21, 62
Mett estate, Canton Vaud	88	New Harmony, Indiana	42
Milbert, Jacques	50	New Jersey	28, 44, 64, 76
Mile Run, Ohio	38	New Jerusalem religion	58
Miller, Adam	48	New Orleans, boat	97
Milwaukee, Wisconsin	30	New Orleans, Louisiana	41, 97
Minamyer, Henry	86	New York (city)	14, 30, 35, 36, 63, 67, 76, 77, 83, 94, 95
Minde, Karl	1		

New York (state) ii, 57, 59
Newfoundland, Canada 26, 36
Nisperley family 64, 89, 90
Nisperly family 64, 89, 90
Noflen, Canton Bern 87
Noll, Samuel 85
Nonenmacher, G.me 70
Nonenmacher, Wilhelm 70
North Carolina ii, 9
Northwest Territory 14, 38
Novo Friburgo, Brazil 5
Nüsperli, Johann Jacob Benedict 89
Nüsperli, Anna Elisabeth "Nanny" 89
Nüsperli, Bendicht 90
Nüsperli, Johann Georg 90
Nüsperli, Ludwig 90
Nüsperli, Maria Magdalena 90
Nüsperli, Samuel 90
Nydegg Church, Bern 86, 91
Nye family ii, 93
Ober-Gerwern society, Bern 9
Obergriesbach, Bavaria 69, 74
Obergruppenbach, Württemberg 74
Oberholzer, Alois 77, 94
Oberholzer, Henry 77
Oberholzer, Ursula 77
Oberholzer family 66, 77, 98
Obermühlern, Canton Bern 88
Obersteckholz, Canton Bern 53
Ohio ii, 9, 13, 16, 41, 66, 82
Ohio Company 38, 66
Ohio River 14, 30, 36, 40, 49, 54, 64, 65, 95, 99
Ohio Township, Monroe County, Ohio 46
Ott, Adolf 53
Oudra, Peter Thomas 77
Paris, France 33
Paris, 2nd Capt. Charles Marie Emmanuel 25
Payerne, Canton Vaud 9, 83, 85
Penn, William 13
Pennsylvania ii, 13, 28, 29, 37, 40, 41, 44, 45, 60, 66, 76, 95
Pennsylvania Inn hotel 65
Perrot, Camille 19
Perth Amboy, New Jersey 27, 44
Peterlingen see Payerne
Pfister, Anna 86
Pfullingen, Württemberg 44, 69
Philadelphia, Pennsylvania 13, 34, 36, 40, 42, 45, 57, 67, 76, 99
Pittsburgh, Pennsylvania 30, 36, 41, 59, 95
Pittsburgh Conference 51
Plainpalais, Geneva, Switzerland 19.
97
Plattenville, Louisiana 20
Platz, C. 42
Platz, Johann Christoph 42
Pletscher, Elisabeth 69
Pletscher, Féréna 69
Pletscher, Martin 69
Pletscher, Verena 69
Point Breeze, New Jersey, estate 44
Port Elizabeth, New Jersey 76
Posey County, Indiana 41
Pot d'Etain, boarding house 42
Powell, Laura Hannah 91
Powhatan Point, Ohio 30, 53, 54
Prince, Charles 78
Princeton, New Jersey 44
Proprietary House, Perth Amboy, New Jersey 28
Prussia 9, 99
Putnam family ii
Putnam, Benjamin Pitt 38
Putnam, David 38
Putnam, General Israel 38
Rabach...see Mömbris-Rappach
Rahm, Melchior 65
Rambler, boat 44
Rapp, Georg 41
Rappach...see Mömbris-Rappach
Reading, Pennsylvania 29
Red River 37, 66
Reiben, now Canton Bern 7, 85
Reichenbach, Albert August 76, 97
Reichenbach, Samuel 15, 16, 40, 41, 76, 97
Reiter, Barbara 70
Reiterinn, Barbe 70
Resecker 64
Retzefeld, Germany 44, 69, 74
Retzefile, Germany 69, 74
Rheindiebach, Rhineland 34
Rhine River 12, 13, 21, 34, 37, 60, 65, 99
Rhodes, Mary Ellen 85
Richard, --, Pastor 85
Richenbach...see Reichenbach
Riehl, Philipp(e) 69
Riemenschneider, Engelhardt 51, 53
Rio Grande, boat 97
Ritzenfeld 44, 69, 74
Ritzrow, Capt. 41, 42
Robespierre 16
Rohrbach, Lewis Bunker 1
Rohrbaugh,..see Rohrbach
Rosenau colony 15, 65
Roth, Anna 86
Röthenbach im Emmental, Canton Bern 90, 91
Rotterdam 13
Rüderswil, Canton Bern 89
Rüderswyl...see Rüderswyl,
Rudin, Theodore, Pastor 54
Rüegsau, Canton Bern 93, 94, 96
Rüegsegger, Anna Margaretha 82, 88, 91
Rüegsegger, Barbara 91
Rüegsegger, Christen 31, 90, 91
Rüegsegger, Christen jr. 90
Rüegsegger, Elisabeth 90

Rüegsegger, Friederich	91	Separatists	21, 41, 42, 61
Rüegsegger, Johannes	90	Seven Ranges	31
Rüegsegger, Niclaus	91	Sicily, Italy	44
Rüegsegger, Peter	91	Simon, Catharina	91
Rüegsegger, Samuel	90, 91	Smith, Priscilla	86
Rüegsegger, Susanna	91	Sohlingen, Germany	68, 74
Rüegsegger, Ulrich	91	Solingen, Germany	74
Ruegsegger family	64	Solothurn, canton	85
Rügsegger...see Rüegsegger		Somerset, Pennsylvania	29
Rüffli, Maria Magdalena	90	Sommer, Isaac	17
Rumpf, Jacob	29	Sonne(n)berg, Ohio	17
Rüschegg, Canton Bern	90	Soumiswald...see Sumiswald	
Rush, Dr. Benjamin	ii	Spaar, Anna Barbara	89
Russia	33	Spain	34, 44
Ruzchak-Eckman, Jeanne	42	Spittler, François	63, 73, 86
Ryffersegg, Röthenbach	90, 91	Spittler, Franz	63, 73, 86
St. Elizabeth Parish, Louisiana	20	Spittler, Sophie	70, 87
St. John's Evangelical Church, Powhatan Point, Ohio	53	Sproat family	ii
		Sproat, Earl	33
St. Louis, Missouri	93	Sproat, Ebenezer	33
St. Martin Parish, Louisiana	19	Spycher, Johannes	91
Salem Township, Monroe County, Ohio	52, 55	Stalder, Andreas	96
		Stalder, Andrew	77
Salzmann, Peter	90	Stalder, Anna	77
Sampson and the Lion, inn, Pennsylvania	44	Stalder, Anna Barbara	94
Sardis, Ohio	55	Stalder, Barbara	96
Schaeffer, Marg.te	70	Stalder, Catharina	94, 95
Schaffhausen...see Schafhouse		Stalder, Catharine	77
Schafhouse, Switzerland	69, 73, 74, 78	Stalder, Christen	94
Schalunen, Canton Bern	83	Stalder, David	94
Scharin, Christian	90	Stalder, Elisabeth	77
Schmid, Johann Jacob	90	Stalder, Frederick	77
Schmidt, Louis	73	Stalder, Friedrich	95
Schmidt, Ludwig	73	Stalder, Georges	77
Schneeder...see Schneider		Stalder, Hans Ulrich	94
Schneider, Barbe	72	Stalder, Jacob	11. 39, 77, 93, 94
Schneider, Bendicht	31, 72, 80, 89		
Schneider, Bendicht Jr.	72, 89	Stalder, Jakob	95
Schneider, Bénoit	72	Stalder, Kaspar	96
Schneider, Bénoit Jr.	72	Stalder, Magdalena	11, 60, 66, 76, 93, 94, 97, 98
Schneider, Elisabeth	89		
Schneider, Elise	72	Stalder, Maria	95
Schneider, Hans	6	Stalder, Nicolas	77
Schncider, J.ques	72	Stalder, Niklaus	96
Schneider, Jakob	72, 89	Stalder, Peter	77, 95
Schneider, Jean	73	Stalder, Rosina	77, 95
Schneider, Johann	73	Stalder, Samuel	94
Schneider, Johannes	6, 82, 89	Stalder, Ursula	94
Schneider, Joseph	89	Stalder, Verena	94
Schneider, Madel.ne	73	Stalder family	66, 93, 97
Schneider, Magdalena	73	Stallaeis	71
Schoray	69, 70, 74	Stamm, Christine	73
Schoulstew, C.	36	Stamm, Férena	73
Schozach	69, 70, 73, 74	Stamm, Jean	73
Schrag, Benedict	17	Stamm, Johann	73
Schtalder...see Stalder		Stamm, Louis	73
Schwarzenberg, Canton Bern	49	Stamm, Ludwig	73
Schweizer, Anna	94	Stamm, Madelaine	· 73
Schweppe, Henry F.	31	Stamm, Madelaine Jr.	73
Sebel family	88	Stamm, Madeleine	73
Sebel, Maria	88	Stamm, Magdalena	73

Stamm, Magdalena Jr.	73	Thurnen, Canton Bern	87
Stamm, Verena	73	Thuun, Daniel, Chaplain	58, 59
Stark County, Ohio	53	Tisher, Jacob	i, 6, 10, 16, 17, 49, 51, 48, 52, 64, 83
Steffisburg, Canton Bern	87, 90		
Steiger, Christoph von	9	Tisher, Jacob...see also Tüscher, Jakob	
Steiger, Elisabeth	76	Tisher family	64, 97
Steiger, Elisabeth von	60	Toggenburger Museum	4
Steiger, Elisabetha Magdalena	93	Tonneins, Guyenne, France	18, 97
Steiger, Emanuel	9	Tompkins, Daniel	ii, 27
Steiger, Johann Rudolph	93	Trachselwald, Canton Bern	86, 93
Steiger, Magdalena von...see Stalder, Magdalena		Trenton, New Jersey	44
		Treves...see Trier	
Steiger, Niklaus Friedrich von	11, 57	Trier	12, 13, 14, 45, 60, 68, 74
Steiger, Rudolph (Freiherr) von	i, 9, 10, 11, 14, 15, 16, 33, 34, 36, 38, 39, 40, 57, 59, 66, 76, 92, 98, 99		
		Trub, Canton Bern	54, 70, 71, 85, 87, 89, 91, 92, 97
Steiger, Rudolph Jr.	76	Tschäppät(t)...see Tschappat	
Steiger, Wilhelmine	76, 92	Tschappat family	64, 72, 97
Steiger de Gran(d)son, von, family	57, 92, 97, 98	Tschappat, [Barbara]	29, 72
		Tschappat, "Bonaparte"	88
Steigersruh, Ohio	38, 59	Tschappat, Cath.e	72
Stein, Meiringen, Canton Bern	84	Tschappat, Catharina	89
Sterchi, Anna	83	Tschappat, Fréd.ck	72
Stettler, Edmnd	92	Tschappat, Friedrich	88
Stettler, Eugen Rudolf	92	Tschappat, J.ques	72
Stettler, Karl Sigmund	92	Tschappat, [Jacob]	72, 88
Stettler, Maria Wilhelmine	92	Tschappat, Jacob Jr.	88
Stettler, Louise	92	Tschappat, Johannes Emanuel	88
Stettler, Samuel	9, 92	Tschappat, M.ie Anne	72
Stick War, Switzerland	2	Tschappat, Marianne	88
Stilli, Canton Aargau	37, 95	Tschappat, Susanna	88
Strasbourg, France	9	Tscharner, von	8
Strickhof, institute	55	Tubaugh...see also Dubach	
Stuttgart, Württemberg	49	Tubaugh, Rosanna	85
Suchard, Philippe	ii, 59	Tupper family	ii
Sulzbach	74	Tupper, Edward White	40
Sumbawa Island	3	Tuscarawas County, Ohio	41, 53
Sumiswald, Canton Bern	77, 78, 94, 96	Tüscher, Abraham	47, 63, 71, 80, 84, 86, 97
Suter...see also Sutter			
Suter, Johann Durs	85	Tüscher, Anna	6, 85
Sutter family	78	Tüscher, Anne	71
Sutter, Jacob	77	Tuscher, Cath.e	71
Sutter, Johann Jakob	95	Tüscher, Catharina	71
Sürvilliers, Count	44	Tuscher, Catharine	84
Susquehanna River	65	Tüscher, Christian	62, 82, 85
Swahlen, John	49	Tüscher, Elisabeth	86
Swedenborgian religion	58	Tüscher, Elise	71
Swiss Confederation	2	Tüscher, Elizab.	71
Swiss Guard	9	Tüscher, Hans	6
Swiss Hills Career Center	55	Tuscher, J.ques (3)	71
Swiss Valley Associates	55	Tuscher, J.ques jr.	71
Switzer, Monroe County, Ohio	55	Tüscher, Jakob	6, 10, 16, 21, 27, 29, 30, 31, 46, 47, 63, 64, 71, 79, 82, 83, 85, 91, 99
Switzerland of Ohio School District	55		
Switzerland Township, Monroe County, Ohio 46, 55			
		Tüscher, Jakob...see also Tisher, Jacob	
Syndonia, boat	97	Tüscher, Jakob jr.	71
Tambora volcano, Indonesia	3	Tuscher, Jean	71
Taylor & Wilder	36	Tuscher, Jeanne Marie	85
Tell, Wilhelm	1	Tüscher, Johannes	71, 85
Texel, Netherlands	63, 94, 99	Tüscher, Maria	71, 85
Thune, Daniel,Chaplain	58, 59	Tüscher, Maria Anna	86

Tuscher, Marie	71	
Tüscher, N.as	71	
Tüscher, Nicklaus	85	
Tüscher, Niklaus	7, 71, 83	
Twan...see Twann		
Twann, Canton Bern	70, 72, 74, 86	
Uhl, David	38, 92	
Uhl, Georg David	92	
Uhl family	97	
Untereisesheim, Württemberg	69, 70, 74	
Unterreisersheim	69, 70, 74	
Vandalia, Illinois	17	
Vanderbilt, Cornelius	ii, 44	
VanderVliet, F.ois	69	
Verret, Marguerite	19	
Vasserot...see Wasserroth		
Vienna, Austria	2, 5	
Vincy, Canton Vaud	16	
Virginia	ii, 16, 30, 51	
Voegtly, Martin	85	
von Fürstenwärther...see Fürstenwärther		
von Gagern...see Gagern		
von Graffenried...see Graffenried		
von Grüningen...see Grüningen		
von Haller...see Haller		
von Steiger...see Steiger		
von Tscharner...see Tscharner		
von Vasserot...see Vasserot		
von Wasserroth...see Wasserroth		
von Wattenwyl...see Wattenwyl		
von Wied-Neuwied...see Wied-Neuwied		
Vuille, August	83, 84	
Wabash River	42	
Wahli, Maria	87	
Walder, G.me	68	
Walder, Wilhelm	68	
Walter, Bern(h)ard	78, 96	
Wangen an der Aare, Canton Bern	84	
Wangenried, Canton Bern	84	
Warden & Brothers	36	
Washington, George, President	ii, 30	
Washington, Pennsylvania	29	
Washington County, Ohio	39, 93, 98	
Wasserroth, (Baron) August von	15	
Wattenwyl, von, family	8	
Wayne County, Ohio	17	
Webel...see Weibel		
Weibel, Anna	78	
Weibel, Johann	96	
Weibel, Johann Rudolph	96	
Weibel, John	78	
Weibel, Maria	78, 96	
Weibel, Rudolph	78	
Weibel, Rudolph jr.	78, 96	
Weimar, Saxony	44, 68	
Weis, Jacob	95	
Weis...see also Wyss		
Weiss, Jacob	78	
Weiss family...see also Wyss	59	
Wengi, Canton Bern	59	
(West) Virginia	ii, 29, 51, 55, 64	
Wetter, Barbara	95	
Wetzel County, (West) Virginia	65, 97	
Weyeneth, Bendicht	54	
Wheeling, (West) Virginia	30, 31, 49	
Whitewater River	66	
Wied-Neuwied, Germany	ii, 40	
Wiessel, Pierre	69	
Wiestling, John	65	
Will(e)wers(ch), Jakob Josef	14, 25	
Will(e)wers(ch), Maria Anna	41, 68	
Williams, Henry J.	40, 41	
Winesburg, Holmes County, Ohio		91
Wintemberg, Rachel	28	
Winter's Grant, Arkansas Territory		41
Winterberger, Catharina...see Katharina		
Winterberger, Ernst	84	
Winterberger, Katharina	7, 46, 84, 91	
Winzenried, Anna	94	
Wissel, Peter	44, 69	
Witmer's Tavern, Pennsylvania	43, 44	
Witschey markets, Ohio	55	
Witzmann, Jacob	42	
Wizemann, Jacob	42	
Wood County, Virginia	92, 97	
Wood County, West Virginia	92, 97	
Worb, Canton Bern	86	
Wright, Frances	64	
Württemberg	21, 42, 44	
Wyss, Elisabeth	59	
Wyss, Jacob	95	
Wyss family	59, 66, 97	
Zaugg, Anna Barbara	92	
Ziegler, Georg	65	
Zimisswald...see Zimmerwald		
Zimmerwald, Canton Bern	71, 74, 88	
Zion Church, Ohio	52	
Zoar, Ohio	42	
Zofingen, Canton Aargau	94	
Zoll, Elise	70	
Zoll, Fréderick	70	
Zoll, Friedrich	70	
Zoll, J.ques (2)	70	
Zoll, Jakob (2)	70	
Zollikofen, Canton Bern	91	
Zschokke, Heinrich	2, 89	
Zuber, Christian	94	
Zürich, canton	55	
Zürich, Switzerland	51, 95	
Zwahlen, John	51	

www.ingramcontent.com/pod-product-compliance
Lightning Source LLC
Chambersburg PA
CBHW051945160426
43198CB00013B/2307